A NATURALIST'S GUIDE
TO GRAND TETON AND
YELLOWSTONE NATIONAL PARKS

FRANK C. CRAIGHEAD JR.

FALCONGUIDES®

GUILFORD, CONNECTICUT
HELENA, MONTANA

AN IMPRINT OF THE GLOBE PEQUOT PRESS

All photos are by Frank C. Craighead Jr., Ph.D., unless otherwise credited.

Library of Congress Cataloging-in-Publication Data is available.

ISBN 978-0-7627-4023-9

Printed in Korea
Revised Edition/Second Printing

All things by almighty power

Near and far

Hiddenly to each other, connected are

That thou cans't not stir a flower

Without the troubling of a star.

Francis Thompson

CONTENTS

PREFACE

Back as far as my grade-school years, while hiking with my father, I recall the questions that, in one form or another, were repeated again and again: "What's the name of that yellow flower?"

"Dogtooth violet."

"Right. Do you remember the name of the bush beside it, the one with the tiny yellow flowers?" No reply. "Here, try chewing the bark."

"Oh!" with no hesitation, "spice bush."

"How about the little purple flower right at your feet?"

"Violet."

"And the tree with the rough bark?"

"Shagbark hickory."

"And the large tree with the hollow trunk?"

"Basswood."

"Correct. The hollow is a result of a heart rot or fungus. These cavities often provide daytime retreats for racoons. Rap on the tree with a stick."

There was a scrambling-like sound from inside the hollow as a large barred owl exploded out of the opening. Shinnying up the tree, I looked down on three young owls and a pile of dead mice, rodents that the parents had caught. The stash of mice, obviously more food than the young birds could eat, was, my father said, an indicator of high rodent populations.

Through many such outings, my brother, sister, and I came to know and enjoy the natural environment around us, whether it was the Potomac River near Washington, D.C., the second-growth, oak-hickory woodlots of southern Michigan, or the spruce-fir forests of the Rocky Mountains.

In this way, I learned the names of many of the birds, mammals, trees, and flowers–the fauna and flora of my immediate environment. When something was of special interest, I dated and recorded the event in a pocket notebook, this along with pertinent data on temperature and weather conditions. Regularly, I noted and recorded concurrent seasonal events. I encouraged my children to do the same, and now I notice that my grandchildren are following suit. This is satisfying for me to see because it's important to start early to teach children how to appreciate, enjoy, and protect the natural environment.

Also, graduate students who have worked for me on various research projects have found it valuable to keep brief field diaries in addition to filling out more formal data sheets.

You may also enjoy using the data provided by this book or your own notes to predict when a specific event may occur and where it fits into the annual sequence of events–for everything there is a season. If the event occurs earlier or later than anticipated from the base data provided in the book, you can try to determine the influencing factors–for everything there is a reason.

You may marvel at the precision with which an individual bird or a particular species shows up at the same nesting site year after year, within days of the same time. Is there an order inherent to the natural world, or is this something that we, as observers and interpreters, must provide? This book and your own experiences may help you find some answers. The results of this approach to taking field notes may help provide insight into the interrelation of events and the interdependence of life forms on one another.

Frank C. Craighead, Jr., Ph.D.
Moose, Wyoming

As I look over this manuscript, I am impressed by the fact that it emerges as a family effort. The help of my wife, Shirley, has been indispensable. Her contributions range from keen observations to skill with the word processor and good judgment in the selection of illustrations. Her enthusiasm for the project and her encouragement to keep at it have given me renewed energy when I most needed it.

There has been the background of information to draw on acquired while collaborating with my brother John.

My sons, Lance and Charles, as well as my daughter, Jana, have grown up under the influence of the little pocket notebook. Knowing in a general way what I have been working on, they have contributed pertinent information, illustrations, and both solicited and unsolicited suggestions and citicism. Their cousin, Craig George, falls into this category, and I thank him as well, for some excellent suggestions.

I have been given encouragement and help by personnel from Grand Teton and Yellowstone National Parks. Terry McEneany, ornithologist for Yellowstone and author of several books relative to the subject, carefully read the manuscript and offered constructive suggestions regarding birds of the area and changes in nomenclature.

Katie Duffy, Park Service Naturalist at Grand Teton National Park, expressed enthusiasm for the manuscript and also offered editorial changes and factual information that improved the text.

I would like to thank the late Joe Murphy, summer park naturalist at Grand Teton and former professor of ecology at Utah State University, for his reading of the text and his encouragement to keep at it.

I appreciate the contribution of credited photographs by Tom Mangelson, Michael S. Sample, Jana C. Smith, Lance Craighead, Shirley Craighead, and Jeffrey T. Hogan.

I am grateful to Chris Cauble, Megan Hiller, and Jeff Wincapaw of Falcon Press Publishing Company for their keen interest in the book and their attention to detail as the finished product emerged under their guidance and care.

I am also grateful to my many friends and acquaintances for their expressed interest and enthusiasm over the years I've been working on this book. I hope that it will be up to their expectations and provide some of the information they have been seeking relative to the total environment of which we are all a part.

—Frank C. Craighead Jr., 1994

Grand Canyon of the Yellowstone

INTRODUCTION

The study of natural phenomena that recur periodically, such as bird migration and nesting, mammal mating and whelping, flowering of plants, leafing of trees, ripening of fruit, coloring of leaves, and the relation of these to climate and changing seasons, is the subject of phenology. This book is based on such phenological observations recorded over forty years in the Teton-Yellowstone area. It is designed to increase your knowledge and enjoyment of the entire northern Rocky Mountain region.

This book has two principal objectives:

1) to provide specific information concerning the *timing* of annual natural events in the Greater Yellowstone Country or ecosystem so that the reader can use this nature calendar to tell when to look for the appearance of concurrent seasonal events—the relation in time of one event to another. Records of this kind serve to inform the bird watcher, for example, that certain nesting activities, such as the fledging of great horned owls, occurs at a time when specific plants like arrowleaf balsamroot are at the peak of flowering or serviceberry is first blooming. You can expect to see one- or two-day old Canada goose goslings when yellow-flowered groundsel first blooms and narrow-leaf cottonwood catkins appear. Conversely, you can look for and expect to see the groundsel in bloom when Canada goose goslings appear. You don't have to rely on calendar dates that may vary from year to year with weather conditions, but you can utilize the occurrence of one event to indicate or to predict another.

2) to provide a phenological method or approach to studying field ecology in the Rocky Mountain area using this book plus existing field guides. This is not a book for the identification of species but rather a guide to a method of learning, enjoying, or teaching field ecology.

The phenological approach to the study of field ecology tends to put one in empathy with the natural environment and reveal the interrelationship of living things with one another. This book is written more for the lay person than the professional. Species identification using other field guides is essential. Here the emphasis is placed on the timing of concurrent events as related to one another in order to locate, observe, and study plants and animals. Phenology relies on the fact that these natural events follow a regular and dependable sequence. This annual sequence of phenological events is established by climate, but the timing of events in relation to calendar days is greatly influenced by local and regional weather conditions. This book should be particularly useful and of interest to the residents of the Greater Yellowstone Ecosystem, the over three million visitors (tourists, hunters, anglers, boaters, photographers, artists, climbers, hikers, and campers) to this area, and to all those to whom increased knowledge of the natural environment adds pleasure to everyday living.

Phenological data have been employed for centuries by farmers who still use events in nature, such as the size of acorns, the snow line on nearby mountains, and the appearance or disappearance of certain flowers, to determine their dates for planting and harvesting certain crops. These natural occurrences, such as first blooming or

peak of flowering of specific plants, can be a more accurate indicator of natural history events than are calendar dates. The first
phenological calendar was compiled 2,500 years ago in China from
annual observations of cherry trees. The longest period of observation was 1,200 years.

THE BASE AREA: MOOSE, WYOMING

Phenological observations of the greatest interest and comparative value are those recorded from the same local area year after
year and throughout the year. This local area is referred to as the
base area. It is usually, as in this case, rather small or limited in size.
The information gathered and presented here is the data base. This
book, a naturalist's field guide, has been compiled from accumulated notes, recorded with varying degrees of completeness over
more than forty years. The nucleus of the base area is the vicinity
of Moose, Wyoming, (6,500 feet), including the Grand Teton
National Park headquarters. The base area embraces Jackson Hole
north, south, east, and west of this center—land that is roughly at
an altitude between 6,000 and 8,000 feet, with 6,500 feet being
considered the base elevation for purposes of comparison. It is
within the Canadian zone which includes plant communities or
vegetative types consisting of spruce-fir, lodgepole pine, sagebrush,
aspen, cottonwood, grassland, and willow-sedge.

The information obtained at the base area has application over
a much larger region, for example, the Greater Yellowstone Ecosystem, and to a lesser degree, the northern and southern Rocky
Mountains. The Greater Yellowstone area consists of parts of seven

national forests, two national parks, three federal refuges, Bureau of Land Management lands, and some state lands in Wyoming, Idaho, and Montana. The time of occurrence of periodic natural history events, such as blooming of certain flowers, when known for the base area, can, by inference, be predicted for other locations and times. From the base area the same events occur *later* as you go north or increase in altitude in spring and summer but occur *earlier* in late summer and autumn as you go northward and higher.

GREATER YELLOWSTONE AREA MAP

The base area studied was Moose, Wyoming, in Grand Teton National Park. The observations and relationships throughout the book can be readily applied to the Greater Yellowstone area and, with adjustments made for latitude and altitude, the entire northern Rocky Mountain region.

GREATER YELLOWSTONE AREA

Legend:
- NATIONAL FOREST
- NATIONAL PARK
- NATIONAL WILDLIFE REFUGE

DEERLODGE NATIONAL FOREST

BEAVERHEAD NATIONAL FOREST

BOZEMAN

GALLATIN NATIONAL FOREST

Madison River

Gallatin River

Yellowstone River

89

191

287

CUSTER NATIONAL FOREST

BEARTOOTH RANGE

RED LODGE

GARDINER

COOKE CITY

MONTANA
WYOMING

45°   45°

212

Clark's Fork of the Yellowstone River

BEAVERHEAD NATIONAL FOREST

RED ROCK LAKES NATIONAL WILDLIFE REFUGE

Yellowstone Canyon

MONTANA
IDAHO

20

WEST YELLOWSTONE

YELLOWSTONE NATIONAL PARK

20

OLD FAITHFUL

SHOSHONE NATIONAL FOREST

TARGHEE NATIONAL FOREST

89
287

Yellowstone Lake

IDAHO
WYOMING

South Fork Shoshone River

44°   44°

JOHN D ROCKEFELLER JR MEMORIAL PARKWAY

Jackson Lake

BRIDGER-TETON NATIONAL FOREST

20

GRAND TETON NATIONAL PARK

MORAN JCT.

Snake River

MOOSE

NATIONAL ELK REFUGE

WIND RIVER RANGE

IDAHO FALLS

Snake River

26

JACKSON

Green River

26
287

CARIBOU NATIONAL FOREST

26
89

187
189

Grays Lake

N

0 2 4 6 8 10   20
Scale in approximate miles

187

189

PINEDALE

How To Use This Guide

For practical purposes, the yearly sequence of events has been divided into weekly units, beginning with the first day of the calendar year. Each dated period is described by a short paragraph set off at its beginning. The period is characterized in terms of easily observed, time-related events. In the case of plants, it is usually the first flowering or the peak of blooming that has been recorded. These dated, seven-day periods, with their accompanying phenological information, help readers orient themselves in their current time frame or in one in which they are interested. For example, June 19-25 near Moose, Wyoming, is about the time pronghorns are giving birth to young and the first yellow flowers of hawksbeard appear. In this way readers can orient themselves in the ongoing sequence of events and thus determine whether their current calendar year is ahead, behind, or synchronous with the phenological calendar being described. Readers can also make use of their own phenological observations to put them in tune with what is going on currently in the plant-wildlife environment.

Readers will notice that specific locations are usually not given as to where certain flowers may be found or animal activities can be observed. This is because natural successional changes alter the vegetation over a relatively short period of time. What is growing there today may be gone tomorrow. In addition, such information tends to concentrate visitor use, resulting in a deterioration of local, fragile environments.

The brief beginning section is followed by a description of other activities and events that coincide in time. These have been selected to arouse interest and curiosity about a specific event and to provide information and references that will encourage readers to seek more knowledge of the subject and, where possible, to verify the findings through field observation.

For some weekly periods there is a partial listing of plants or animals that can be easily found. Among these may be a first flowering or an animal activity with which readers are more familiar than with the key phenological examples given. Readers may use these indicators. They'll be easier to relate to and to remember.

APPLICATION OF METHOD

As mentioned earlier in the text, the phenological information in this book is specific for the Greater Yellowstone area, and applicable to a lesser degree to the northern and southern Rocky Mountains, within the spruce-fir zone.

The phenological method of study can be duplicated elsewhere. Perhaps readers might try this out in their home area, such as the Mid-Atlantic states or the Mid-Western region. If readers record and date their observations over a period of time they will create their own field guide.

EQUIPMENT

Readers can make phenological observations as they go about their everyday outdoor activities. No equipment is essential; however, to make it a satisfying and productive hobby, a small pocket notebook, pen, binoculars, and a few field guides and reference books are needed. Some that readers might start with are in the

Peterson series: *A Field Guide to Hawks, A Field Guide to Western Birds, A Field Guide to Rocky Mountain Wildflowers, A Field Guide to Western Butterflies, A Field Guide to the Mammals, North America North of Mexico,* and *A Field Guide to Animal Tracks.* These and other references are given in a list of suggested readings at the end of the book.

Readers' observations can be enhanced and expanded by the use of a spotting scope, an altimeter, a hand magnifying lens, and a thermometer.

Scientific Names

All the plants and animals that you will see have names already assigned to them by taxonomists. All have a Latin or scientific name, genus, species, maybe even subspecies, and most will also have one or more common names. The scientific name of each plant is given when first mentioned in the text. After this, only the common name is used. The scientific and common names of animals mentioned in the text are given in tables at the back of the book. A necessary first step in the learning process is to give correct names to the plants or animals you locate and observe. The identification and naming of what you see can be accomplished by using field guides or, better yet, having a knowledgeable friend point out a particular plant, name it, and perhaps even list a few of the identifying characteristics.

By noting and dating phenological events, readers not only learn to recognize species, but begin to get a feeling for the interrelationships of animals with plants, and the response of both to physical conditions of the environment. The temporary and local influence of weather is seen along with the long range, year- by -year, constant, and consistent effects of climate. This reveals itself in the northern and southern temperate hemispheres as the seasons—spring, summer, fall, and winter.

This phenological approach to studying the relations between life and climate automatically takes into consideration the influence of parameters such as temperature, humidity, wind velocity, sunlight, precipitation, etc., on the growing organism. Because phenology does this, a developing organism is an expression of a broad spectrum of observable environmental effects and variables, only a few of which can be accurately measured with instruments.

We will start with the observation and recording of phenological events beginning with the change of seasons from winter to spring and on into summer and fall. But these seasonal changes and recurring natural history events are cyclic, hence we could start at any time.

According to Andrew D. Hopkins, a noted entomologist and early student of phenology, other things being equal, the time variation in seasonal activities and phenomena is at the average rate of four days difference for each degree of latitude (70 miles), and four days for every 400 feet of altitude (one day per 100 feet of altitude).

The rate of variation in the timing of events is the same with any given combination of altitude and latitude, provided other conditions are equal. Year after year, events will occur in a rough but orderly sequence as established by climate.

Introduction to the Year

In the Greater Yellowstone Country, or ecosystem, December 22, the winter solstice, is a time of low temperatures, penetrating cold, and accumulating snow. The sun reaches its lowest point on the southern horizon. It is the shortest day of the year and the beginning of winter in the northern hemisphere. From this time on, the days progressively lengthen until about March 21 when the sun crosses the plane of the earth's equator making night and day of equal length all over the earth. This, the vernal equinox, marks the beginning of spring. From this time on, the length of the days increase until June 21, the longest day of the year and the time when the sun reaches its northernmost point. As the earth in its orbit revolves around the sun, it is tilted at an angle of 23.5 degrees, always in the same direction in space. This inclination of the earth, along with its revolution around the sun, causes the length of day and night to change and produces the seasons: winter, spring, summer, and fall; each of which is characterized and fashioned by distinctive and recognizable climatic conditions for any given area. The regularity of the appearance of the seasons each year is consistent, as is the life activity and phenomena that accompanies and characterizes each season.

Following the winter solstice, the days lengthen, but severe winter conditions persist and increase. The landscape is snow-covered; temperatures drop well below zero and remain there for weeks at a time. Winter birds, such as common ravens, bald eagles, mountain and black-capped chickadees, pine grosbeaks, hairy and three-toed woodpeckers, gray jays, Clark's nutcrackers, black-billed magpies, and red-breasted nuthatches, are present in suitable habitats, but reduce their activity in order to conserve body heat through the use of various heat-saving adaptations. During the month of January, winter conditions still dominate. An overall whiteness prevails, broken only by the dark green of coniferous trees. Rock faces and outcrops are intermittently scoured or snow-plastered by chilling winds.

Through early February full winter conditions still predominate. It is a cold, hostile environment, but on clear sunny days the careful observer will see the first signs of the approach of spring. During the brief intervals of warmer weather, ravens will be seen flying in pairs. The pairs become more and more evident as winter wanes. You may also see them perched side by side for long periods of time, one bird sometimes briefly preening the other. Great horned owls may occasionally be heard hooting, sometimes followed by an answering hoot, the tenuous beginning of courtship. During the latter part of February, paired ravens are observed more frequently, and the courtship hooting of horned owls is heard more often. On warm and sunny days, bird activities increase, followed by a regression to winter inactivity on wintry, stormy days. These subtle changes in bird activity are the first indicators that once again spring will replace winter, and a well-defined sequence of events among plant and animal life will take place.

Grand Teton, Mount Owen, Mount Teewinot

*The shortest day of the year (December 21)
has come and gone with the severest winter
weather still ahead, but the shortest,
dark days are behind.*

ONE OF THE FIRST bird species to re-establish and passively defend a nesting territory will be the ravens. Paired ravens may be seen sitting side by side on days when the weather is fair and their appetites satisfied, a situation that occurs more frequently as spring evolves. With spring in the air and time to spare, the ravens play, a luxury most species do not have. Red crossbills may initiate nesting during any month of the year. Boreal and great horned owls may be heard calling, this being their courtship period.

At the end of February and during the first days of March, ravens and Canada geese are seen more frequently in pairs with sporadic defense of nest sites by geese. Possible sighting of an early arriving mountain bluebird, an event eagerly anticipated by bird watchers.

SOME EARLY nesting bald eagles may start laying eggs, and ravens are performing courtship flights on sunny, spring-like days. You can see the ravens chase one another, dropping from on high in falcon-like stoops, one bird close behind the other. This is combined with rolls and loops, some while skimming the ground, and others while playfully riding the air currents or challenging the gusty gales. When not flying, pairs perched close together may be seen preening each other's feathers. At the same time, Canada geese return to claim old (or select new) nesting territories, honking defensively at intruders. A few that have remained throughout the winter now fly in pairs, as do the trumpeter swans, seeking ice-free water. This is also the time when you can expect to see one of the first spring migrants, the mountain bluebird, the bright blue of the male easily discernable against a background of dazzling white snow.

Mountain Bluebird

Coincident with the arrival of mountain bluebirds is the appearance of a few midges (snow mosquitoes or Chironomids), on the snow-covered banks of the upper Snake and Yellowstone rivers. These insects provide food for the early arriving bluebirds and for the trout and Rocky Mountain whitefish as well. Their numbers will increase as the days get warmer. When wintry March conditions prevail, creating a "late spring," the snow midges will not emerge and the bluebirds, perhaps along with a lone red-winged blackbird or two, will disappear to return later under more clement conditions and in greater numbers. Anglers will do well to follow their example. Some years the robins and Cassin's finches show up simultaneously with the mountain bluebirds.

The landscape is largely snow-covered, but there will be scattered patches of bare ground under spruce and fir trees providing feeding sites for the arriving robins as well as for winter residents such as chickadees. Horned larks and rosy finches may appear while Clark's nutcrackers move from winter areas to nesting sites. Territorial golden eagles are performing their undulating courtship flights at a time when migrating golden eagles are moving northward through Greater Yellowstone.

*A slow or rapid increase in number of
bird migrants, depending on weather.
American robins and male red-winged blackbirds
appearing with the first sign of changes in
plant life, the noticeable enlarging of aspen
and broadleaf cottonwood flower buds.
Great horned owls are laying eggs.*

DURING THE SECOND week in March of an early spring, a few red-tailed hawks may make an appearance in lower Jackson Hole, having moved up from Afton and Alpine, Wyoming. At about the same time, red-winged blackbirds, dark-eyed (Oregon or pink-sided) juncos, robins, European starlings, rosy finches, Cassin's finches, and Brewer's blackbirds will show up at higher elevations and further north. Due to the vagaries of weather, the appearance of these early arrivals may vary by as much as a month from one year to the next. Great horned owls may be found together—the male perching alone, the female in a nearby hollow tree, laying eggs or incubating. Insects such as flies, and spiders are active during warm days on grass or earth heated by the sun. At this time you may observe the first appearance of the red admiral, a butterfly whose larvae feed on the

LANCE CRAIGHEAD

Milbert's Tortoiseshell Butterfly

young buds and leaves of the stinging nettle (*Urtica dioica*). This nettle may be the first spring green growth you will see. Once you identify young nettle leaves, a little time spent in their vicinity may provide you with your first sighting of a red admiral or a Milbert's tortoiseshell butterfly, likewise feeding on the nettles. The young plants indicate the possible presence of the butterflies, and either butterfly is a clue to locating emerging nettles, the young leaves of which can be boiled to provide a tasty spring potherb.

Up until this time the signs of approaching spring are mainly visible in bird behavior (singing, pairing, courtship, territorial defense) and in the arrival of migrants returning to nesting sites; first a few and then in growing numbers, increasing from lone individuals to flocks (juncos, blackbirds, finches, robins, bluebirds).

During this period in March when spots of bare ground are showing but with still much snow around, you can detect an en–larging and opening of the catkin buds of the aspen *(Populus tremuloides)* and the enlarging of the leaf buds of the narrowleaf

Starling

cottonwood (*Populus angustifolia*). Inclement weather may retard further development for weeks or more; sunny warm days stimulate further growth. As an example, at the base area, the spring of 1991 seemed destined to be an early one as warm temperatures encouraged the opening of aspen flower buds by March 12. Cold weather and snow storms followed. A month later (April 13), there was no noticeable change in the development of aspen catkins. Plant life in general had remained relatively dormant for a full month.

TOM MANGELSEN

Red-winged Blackbird

When the snow disappears creating an early spring, Clark's nutcrackers will have completed nest building and may be laying eggs. Robins and mountain bluebirds are increasing in numbers and the males are establishing or claiming nesting territories. This at the time when the earliest blooms of the inconspicuous Indian potato plant appear.

IT IS NOT UNTIL you see the white fluffy male catkins of the willows *(Salicaceae)* or the tiny white flowers of the Indian potato plant *(Orogenia linearifolia)* that you can say spring has arrived. Indian potato plant, growing in relatively bare patches of ground among the sagebrush, is difficult to see. Its linear leaves, grass-like in appearance, will help you locate it. Look for both of these announcers of spring at about the time of the spring equinox (March 20, 21). Some of the earliest flowering plants include the cottonwoods, aspens and poplars (*Populus*), and the willows. Two types of flowers (aments) are borne on separate trees. The pollen-bearing male flowers on one tree, and the female flowers developing into seeds on another. The small, early-appearing flowers in long clusters are catkins (male). They bloom before the

Elk

MICHAEL S. SAMPLE

leaves unfold. The seeds, which also appear in spring, but later than the male catkins, bear white cottony hairs (cottonwood fluff) used to disperse the seeds. Cottonwood and aspen catkins hang down; those of the willow are upright.

With the appearance of aspen catkins, starlings are arriving and feeding in flocks rather than singly or in pairs, as is the case with other first arrivals. A welcome food bonanza for the early arriving starlings is the masses of wood ticks which they greedily pick off sick and dying moose, elk, and bison—casualties of the winter.

Mountain bluebirds are now exploring possible nesting sites—hollows in trees, fence posts, holes made by flickers or sapsuckers, and even cracks in houses.

Great horned owls have settled on a nest site, very often one used the year before—an old hawk or raven stick nest, a well-protected ledge on a rocky cliff, or a snug hollow in a cottonwood tree. The great horned owls will incubate their white eggs, usually two in number, but sometimes three if the environmental cues for a potential food supply of rodents are good. As they settle down to incubate their eggs, there is sufficient bare ground for the owls to hunt rodents made vulnerable by the loss of protective snow cover.

This same bare ground, with last year's dried plants, is sufficient for the elk, some of which now leave the National Elk Refuge in small bands. The elk are sensitive to changing weather patterns, at times moving north to start their spring migration, then moving back as snow storms and inclement weather prevail. It appears as though elk can detect approaching storms early and alter their movements and behavior accordingly. This may be related to the animals' possible ability to detect infrasound waves created by approaching but distant storms. Small bands of elk can be seen over a period of weeks moving out, then returning, in response to advance storm warnings. Eventually, they head north, many moving past Kelly, Wyoming, leaving Jackson Hole and traveling higher and northward as the snow-line recedes to expose the scarce but new green growth.

Great Horned Owl

Early arriving red-tailed and Swainson's hawks establish or lay claim to nesting territories by circling or soaring overhead. Sometimes vocal threats are needed to repel intruders, and even outright aerial battles may occur between contending pairs. This time of year, prior to the leafing of trees, nests are being repaired or built anew. It is the best period for locating nesting hawks and ravens. Upon arrival, the hawks soar and circle over, or close to, their nest site. Last year's nest is usually close by. Frequently you can see this nest enlarge as the old nest is refurbished with new sticks. Sometimes the beginning of a new one suddenly appears. By recording early hawk and raven sightings you can reduce the area where you must later hunt for a nest. The task of locating raven, buteo, and accipiter (short-winged hawks) nests becomes much more difficult after the aspens and cottonwoods put out their leaves.

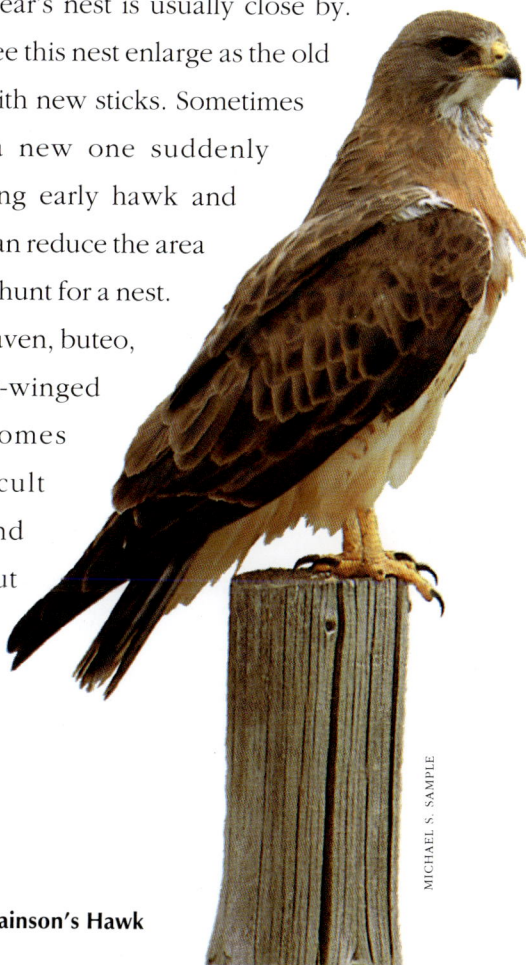

MICHAEL S. SAMPLE

Swainson's Hawk

Aspen and cottonwood buds continue to enlarge, midges increase in numbers and mate. Snow geese are moving through. Ducks, such as green-winged teals, cinnamon teals, and gadwalls show up as water habitats become ice-free. Sandhill cranes arrive. Clark's nutcrackers, gray jays, and great horned owls are incubating eggs. Bald eagles are repairing old nests and starting to lay, or have laid, eggs, usually two.

ON INTO THE NEXT week, animal activities will dominate the scene while plants will change slowly. Aspen, cottonwood, and mountain alder *(Alnus incana)* buds continue swelling and enlarging. Small flocks of cedar waxwings may appear suddenly and just as quickly vanish. An early arriving western meadowlark may be a forerunner of more to come. With a spell of cold weather or a light snow, the early meadowlarks, bluebirds, and red-winged blackbirds may take flight to lower altitudes or to protected areas where bare ground assures at least a meager subsistence. They will return when sun warmth and melting snow again make the habitat hospitable to the northward moving avian populations.

At this time of the spring equinox, when the days start to get progressively longer than the nights, you may hear the calls of the sandhill cranes in flight, often before the birds are seen. Some settle down on ice-bound Grays Lake, in the southwest portion of the ecosystem, while others continue their migration north to Yellowstone and beyond. Still others settle down in their Jackson Hole summer home. Already paired, they soon perform their courtship dances, thus announcing their claim to a former nesting territory. Being more or less at the same altitude and latitude (difference of a half degree north latitude), the spring conditions in Jackson Hole and at Grays Lake National Refuge are comparable—mountain bluebirds, starlings, robins, and red-winged blackbirds have returned.

By now, soil along stream banks or in moist areas has thawed enough by noonday for cranes and robins to feed on earthworms and other soil inhabitants. The midges rise up in ever increasing numbers through snow tunnels and cracks to reach the surface. Here these flies form large hatches of flying insects, the pairs mating, then dropping back to the snow or earth where they are consumed by the growing numbers of hungry bluebirds, robins, and cranes. Midges, though tiny, make up a tremendous volume of food for these migrants and early arrivals.

JANA C. SMITH

Robin

Hawks become more conspicuous, returning as the avian prey base increases, and aspen and willow catkins appear along with the shiny yellow flowers of sagebrush buttercup. In Grand Teton National Park the cutthroat trout fishing season opens, often with considerable snow still covering the banks of the Snake River.

WITH THE FIRST blooming of the sagebrush buttercup *(Ranunculus glaberrimus)*, some years as early as March 27, look for returning hawks. It is a period when northern goshawks and red-tailed hawks may make their first appearance. The goshawks prey on the resident and migrant waterfowl as well as on the increasing numbers of passerine birds. Single red-tailed hawks may be observed, and a few days later pairs will defend nesting territories, especially on warm, sunny days. These birds will generally appear first in the lower parts of Jackson Hole as far down as the confluence of the Hoback and Snake rivers. Over a span of days and weeks they and others will eventually put in an appearance in the vicinity of the Grand Teton National Park headquarters at Moose, Wyoming (altitude 6,500 feet).

Some over-wintering bald and golden eagles will have finished repairing large stick nests and will begin to lay eggs. Golden eagles prefer nest sites such as canyon cliffs with an extensive

Heron Rookery

view or large conifers, perhaps a spreading Douglas fir *(Pseudotsuga menziesii)*. Bald eagles invariably nest in trees where they can see water.

Male kestrels observed during this period in the lower valley may not show up at Moose for another three weeks. Although it is only about 25 miles north, Moose is over 500 feet higher in elevation. At this time of year, black-billed magpies and ravens do some sporadic nest building. Many of the raven nests are lined with horse and cattle hair. Mountain bluebird numbers increase, all actively seeking and appraising nest sites. Canada geese are noisily defending nesting territories and nest sites. Great blue herons are returning to last year's stick nests in the heron rookeries. In most cases, winter winds have made repair mandatory.

Meadowlarks and killdeer put in their first appearance. Red-tailed hawks may be seen copulating, a sign that they will soon be incubating eggs. Male northern harriers (formerly marsh hawks) may tumble into sight as they turn, twist, and dive in a spectacular courtship flight. Rough-legged hawks, when sighted, will be on their way to the far north to complete the nesting phase of their annual cycle. The span of their nesting season will be compressed into a shorter period than that of the buteos nesting at lower latitudes.

As the migrating hawks move northward to take up summer residence in the Greater Yellowstone Country, the first to appear are the red-tailed hawks, followed closely by the Swainson's hawks, then the goshawks, kestrels, northern harriers, prairie falcons, possibly a peregrine falcon or merlin, and finally, the bird-eating accipiters, the Cooper's and sharp-shinned hawks (Table VIII). These, including the golden eagle, bald eagle, and osprey, make up the day-time avian hunters, while the great horned, great gray, long and short-eared, boreal, western screech, northern saw-whet, and northern pygmy- owls make up the avian night hunters. This collective population of nesting

JEFFREY T. HOGAN

Goshawk

16

raptors, some hunting in the daytime, others at night, are each adapted to take certain types of prey and exert hunting pressure on the various prey species whose numbers are rapidly increasing through reproduction. In this way, the combined populations of raptors and mammalian predators reduce and tend to regulate populations of prey species, thus tending to keep their numbers within the carrying capacity of the ecosystem. Normally, a single predatory species, even though abundant, cannot do this.

Colorado and least chipmunks scamper in and out of depleted piles of firewood or brush. They stick close to cover, for at this time they may be particularly vulnerable to predation by hawks. The more numerous Uinta ground squirrels have not yet risen from their underground bed chambers where they have been hibernating during the winter months.

Bird and mammal activities dominate the scene and seem to be turned on and off by weather changes that vacillate between warm sunshine and snow flurries or storms that may cover the ground with three or four inches of new snow. Plant growth is slow, held in check by temporary but adverse weather conditions and a considerable but spotty snow cover. With a few days of consecutive warm weather, a white phlox *(Phlox multiflora)* situated favorably on a south-facing slope may bloom early before others of its kind. Temperature of a microenvironment varies with slope. An incline of as little as 5 degrees toward the north reduces soil temperature about as much as does moving 300 miles of latitude in the same direction.

White Phlox

*Ravens are laying their first eggs, elk are moving
higher as snow recedes. Moose are congregating
in the open to feed on bitterbrush twigs and leaves.
Ground squirrels are emerging from hibernation
to be preyed on by red-tailed hawks, whose
numbers are increasing. The hawks are building
large stick nests. The earliest nesting Canada geese
are laying eggs.*

BY THE FIRST WEEK in April, alder male catkins will start to slowly enlarge, and tiny tips of bitterbrush (*Purshia tridentata*) leaves appear. Moose now leave the willow bottoms and move to the snow-covered sagebrush *(Artemisia tridentata)* flats to feed on bitterbrush, one of their preferred shrubs. The habit makes them quite conspicuous, and at this time they can be readily filmed by photographers. However, care should be taken not to approach too closely. They are dangerous.

There is sufficient bare ground to entice more elk from the southern herd to leave their winter range (the National Elk Refuge). In small bands they move past the north end of Blacktail Butte and on up the valley to the receding snow line where last year's grass provides sustenance until green forage appears. Most of the bull elk have dropped their antlers during the late winter months, but some still carry their racks, losing them as they migrate to higher elevations.

Aspen leaf buds are now noticeably enlarged. These are indicators that early nesting ravens are laying their first greenish-brown eggs, and that osprey are back and defending their nest sites. The first of the yellow-rumped or Audubon's warblers may now be seen. Starlings are flying in small flocks rather than singly.

At about this time a few Canada geese may be laying eggs on island nest sites in the Snake River. The average clutch size is five. The female does all the incubating. Snow depth largely determines the time the geese will start laying each year. If snow lingers on the nesting sites, egg laying will be delayed. When snow-free earth appears, laying will start. Most nests are on islands a few feet above the water level. Nests tend to be located close to brush piles, on gravel bars, or close to patches of vegetation. They are usually lined with down which the goose pulls over

TOM MANGELSEN

Yellow-rumped Warbler

the eggs when she leaves the nest. A few geese utilize old hawk or osprey nests or stubs of broken cottonwoods. Some may be as high as thirty to forty feet above the ground. These elevated nests appear to provide excellent security, some being successfully used year after year for periods of ten years or more.

Over forty years ago (1947), my brother John and I made a census of the nesting population of geese along a section of the Snake River from Moran to Wilson, Wyoming (forty miles). We found that there were between eighty-eight to ninety pairs, based on nest counts made while floating the river. This census has served as baseline data useful in making comparisons with later censuses. Two comparable nesting counts in 1974 and 1979 revealed nesting populations of seventy to seventy-six pairs of geese respectively. The figures, though indicating a decline over periods of twenty-seven to thirty-two years, also suggest a remarkable nesting population

Goose Nest

stability, particularly in view of human impact on the river and its environs—channeling, diking, roading, gravel removal, fishing, recreational boating, and housing developments. The goose

Canada Goose

population stability in turn suggests an amazing ability of Canada geese to adapt to changing conditions. The effect of river channeling and diking on nesting sites should be monitored from time to time. Research data that provides opportunity to compare present conditions with those of the past enable resource managers to initiate, develop, and defend sound management programs.

Sage grouse gather on strutting grounds or leks,
emerging ground squirrels (or chiselers) increase
the availability of prey for nesting raptors—this at
about the same time that grizzly bears leave their
winter dens. Great horned owl eggs are hatching,
and red-tailed hawks are completing nest building.
Northern flickers (red-shafted race), more sandhill
cranes, tree swallows, Cassin's and rosy finches,
and killdeer appear as Indian potato continues
to bloom under the sagebrush.

STEPPING INTO an early departing plane at the Jackson Hole airport, an observant visitor might first hear, then see, strutting male sage grouse inflating their neck sacs, then deflating them with a loud popping or booming noise. This ritual takes place while an audience of inconspicuous females looks on, both here and at other traditional leks throughout the valley. A typical lek is a large, open, grassy arena surrounded by sagebrush. Some leks that I have observed and photographed over forty years ago are still in use today; others have disappeared. At some, close to one hundred birds participated in their early morning rituals. Sage grouse, strutting on the airport site, are in conflict with the alleged need to extend the runway, thus eliminating the lek. Such

MICHAEL S. SAMPLE

Sage Grouse

conflicts over the use of resources can generally be satisfactorily and appropriately resolved if all the facts are considered. However, increasing population growth with the accompanying development makes such decisions ever more frequent and difficult.

The number of birds putting in their first appearance and/or increasing in numbers is rapidly expanding. Robins are nest building when male American kestrels show up in the valley. A few dandelions (*Taraxacum officinale)* may be in bloom. Lance-like leaves of death camas (*Zigadenus paniculatus*) are protruding two to three inches out of the ground and are being clipped by hungry wildlife. A sprinkling of flickers arrive, their undulating flight a contrast to the short, precise wing-beats of the noisy sandhill cranes, now staging courtship dances. In some spring seasons the Moose, Wyoming, base area is largely free of snow, while in other years there is a foot or more still blanketing the protruding sagebrush.

Regardless of the immediate environmental conditions, snow-covered or snow-free, cold or mild, the ground squirrels pop up from hibernation at about the same time each year. Ground Squirrel Day in Jackson Hole was April 5 in 1979, April 11 in '80 and '81, April 4 in '82, April 2 in '86, April 9 in '88, April 6 in '89, April 3 in '91, and April 5 in '92. The emergence of ground squirrels after nine months of hibernation apparently is not influenced as much by environmental conditions as is the emergence of bears. Instead, the ground squirrels awakening from hibernation is controlled by a "physiological clock" within the body that increases their body temperature and steps up their heart rate, thus informing them when to leave their winter beds. If the snow blanket is still deep, they will tunnel three or more feet up to daylight. On the vast expanse of white, their dark bodies are quite conspicuous as they stand upright and then scamper about. The leaves and shiny yellow flowers of sagebrush buttercup sparkle even in the shade. The ground squirrels feed avidly on these early blooming plants. At this time they breed, giving birth to their young a month later (Table VII).

A sign of pocket gophers, earth tailings, is now revealed as the snow melts. Snake-like earth cores, removed when digging tunnels in the earth and under the snow, stand

Uinta Ground Squirrel

out in relief. Pocket gophers, unlike ground squirrels, do not hibernate but remain active in their tunnel systems, eating stored food and roots of herbs, grasses, small trees, and shrubs. After watching a two-foot plant shrink to one foot, you may rub your eyes and look again as the disappearing plant is pulled into the tunnel system by the unseen gophers below.

Dandelion Fields

By the time the first dandelions appear, there is a widely distributed and growing food supply for the increasing numbers of hawks and owls—either nesting or preparing to nest. It is a time when the deer or white-footed mice are giving birth to young. The eggs of the great horned owl are hatching, and the young need a reliable food supply. American crows are back, feeding in small flocks or defending former nest sites, ones not contested by the larger ravens. Bluebirds are now numerous and their food is plentiful—crowded bunches of midges covering rocks in dark masses at the interface of snow and water.

When grizzly bears first emerge from hibernation, the snow is often too soft and deep for them to travel. They may remain close to their dens until mid-April, when warm sunny days followed by chilly nights put a crust on the snow that will support their weight.

Grizzly and Cubs

When new roundstem bulrush (*Scirpus acutus*) shoots are appearing along edges of water courses, the tubers of Indian potato, spring beauty *(Claytonia lanceolata),* and yellow-flowered Wyeth biscuitroot *(Lomatium ambiguum)* are available on snowfree southern exposures. Here, the direct rays of the sun warm the bare soil. Found blooming here at about the same time is the carrot-like-leafed desert-parsley (*Lomatium foeniculaceum*). These plants, as well as carcasses of winter-killed ungulates—elk, bison, moose, and deer—together provide both vegetable and animal food for the hungry adult bears with their new cubs of the year.

*Kestrels and white-crowned sparrows arrive at
former nest sites when aspen catkins are
conspicuous. Their arrival coincides with the first
appearance of yellowbell and spring beauties.
Common snipe are now seen and heard in their
first courtship flights. Elk are still migrating
upward to summer range. Canada geese reach
their peak of egg laying. Common mergansers are
beginning to incubate their large clutches of eggs,
often deposited in tree hollows
or on cliff ledges.*

TO THE OBSERVER, there is still more evidence of spring
from animal activities than from the appearance of plant growth.
Where the ground is bare, look for the first blooming yellowbells
(*Fritillaria pudica*), spring beauties, and steershead (*Dicentra
uniflora*). When they appear, you can expect to see tiercel (male)
kestrels arriving at former nest hollows. Over the years the variation in the arrival time of kestrels and their defense of a former
territory does not vary by more than a few days. This is particularly noticeable among individuals observed over consecutive
years. This punctuality might be taken as an indicator that
the more extreme fluctuations in spring weather conditions are

American Kestrel

smoothing out by the time kestrels arrive. The female regularly arrives later than the male.

Paired starlings have selected nesting hollows in trees and in some cases have usurped nest cavities formerly used by kestrels. They have the advantage of arriving before the kestrels. In 1947 when I first started studying the base area, there were no nesting starlings in Jackson Hole. Now the flocks of juvenile birds raised in the area can be measured in the thousands, giving them the advantage over the kestrels in numbers as well as in timing. The impact of this aggressive, exotic species on the environment should be anticipated and given consideration in future, non-game management plans. The same applies to the crow, once a non-resident, now nesting and flocking in ever-increasing numbers. If continued, what effect might this have on raven or buteo populations?

Osprey have returned from warmer climates and are refurbishing last year's nest in preparation for laying eggs, usually three.

JANA C. SMITH

Raven Eggs

The American wigeon, gadwall, common merganser, bufflehead, lesser yellowlegs, house wren, and great blue heron may all now be seen as well as song sparrows, dark-eyed juncos, American goldfinches, rosy finches, and Cassin's finches (Table II). Warm, sunny spring days encourage the male Cassin's finches to initiate their courtship displays. Standing on a prominent branch, rock, or log, the male rapidly vibrates his wings, much like a ruffed grouse. Picking up a stick and holding it in his bill, he looks up at the female and repeats the performance to an apparently uninterested potential mate. Male bluebirds are flitting about checking out nest cavities. More western meadowlarks, the Wyoming state bird, have re-turned, and the males are singing from conspicuous perches. Townsend's solitaires, sharp-shinned hawks, Cooper's hawks, and Swainson's hawks are just arriving. Mourning doves are back, and the tree swallows are increasing in numbers. About this time you should be able to hear the winnowing sound of the common snipe as the male dives earthward in courtship flight over the wet or marshy breeding areas. If you look carefully toward the source of the sound, which is made by the vibrating tail feathers, you can catch a fleeting glimpse of the snipe in flight. It is truly a spring sound, audible throughout the nesting season—somewhat like a rapid, muffled screech or boreal owl call. Apparently coming from nowhere, it is sometimes a bit eerie.

Downward hanging aspen catkins are now rippling in the wind, but the leaf buds have not yet opened nor have those of the narrowleaf cottonwood. Some erect willow catkins have appeared, but not the leaves. The landscape in general is still wintry in appearance with no sign of greening trees. The leaves of nettle and cow parsnip (*Heracleum sphondylium*) protrude a few inches above ground, but are growing slowly. Wood ticks begin to show up, having transferred from brush to hiker's clothing. They are likely to be more numerous where elk, deer, or moose have bedded down. After a hike it is wise to check yourself for ticks and remove them if crawling or attached. They can transmit the serious Rocky Mountain spotted fever.

When some of the early spring flowers are first appearing and summer bird residents are increasing in numbers, float trips down the Snake River or tributaries will reveal a diversity of wildlife. Float trips can provide the opportunity to make systematic relative abundance counts of the birds or other wildlife seen along a definite stretch of river a quarter mile to either side of the observer. These rough censuses, when made regularly or annually, and under somewhat comparable conditions, can provide you with approximate numbers of birds and mammals present. This information is valuable in revealing present conditions, annual or periodic changes, and even trends in wildlife populations (Table X). The Christmas Bird Count conducted by the National Audubon Society and the Breeding Bird Survey are examples of such counts (Table IX). With global threats to animal and plant diversity resulting in a deteriorating natural environment, it behooves us all to know our environment, to be responsive to the changes occurring, and to evaluate them on a local or even regional basis. The sooner that adverse changes can be detected, the quicker remedial steps can be taken. We can all help, if only in a limited or small way. As *Sky* magazine aptly expressed it, "Think globally, act locally" (April 1993).

Many plants that have flowered earlier continue to bloom. Spring bird migrants already present increase in numbers. Some early arriving robins are laying eggs while ravens are incubating eggs. A few male sage grouse are still strutting, red-tailed and ferruginous hawks are laying eggs, bald eagle and golden eagle eggs have hatched or are hatching, and starlings are nest building at the time of the first flowering of shooting star, star flower, queencup, and yellow violet. An occasional rare whooping crane may stop here briefly during migration to northern nesting sites.

WHITE-CROWNED SPARROWS still show up at former nesting territories. Western meadowlarks, dark-eyed juncos, northern flickers, mountain bluebirds, mourning doves, European starlings, and Cassin's finches become more numerous and attract migrating sharp-shinned hawks, Cooper's hawks, and northern harriers. House finches, pine grosbeaks, yellow-headed blackbirds, brown-headed cowbirds, and evening grosbeaks have appeared. Barrow's goldeneyes, cinnamon and green-winged teals, as well as common mergansers, fly, feed, and cavort in pairs. When you see only single birds, it is an indication that

Bison and Calf

incubation of eggs has begun. Common loons may be seen on lakes that are no longer ice-bound. Bison are calving when both male and female sage grouse disperse from their ancestral strutting grounds to initiate nesting activity. Butterflies, including the red admiral and the mourning cloak, become more numerous.

These events take place as golden willows (*Salix* sp.) unfold their leaves, and small, wedge-shaped leaves of bitterbrush

begin to give a slight, patchy
greenness to the sagebrush
areas where they grow. In wet
habitats or marshy areas, male
alder catkins turn the stream-
side vegetation a brownish-
red as they expand and elon-
gate while emitting pollen. It
is time to look for the first
flowering of the conspicuous,
rose-purple shooting star
(*Dodecatheon pulchellum*),

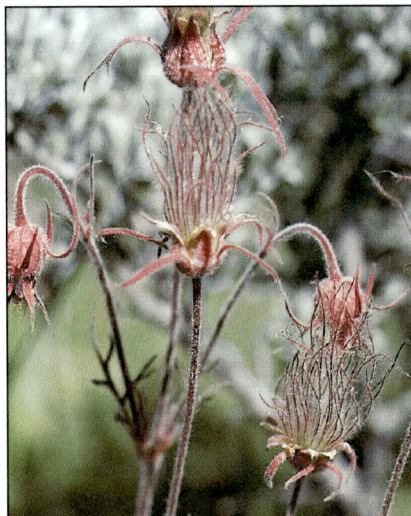

Long-plumed Avens

the tiny blue-lips (*Collinsia parviflora*), the dainty star flower
(*Lithophragma parviflorum*), queencup (*Clintonia uniflora*),
yellow violet (*Viola nuttallii*), and the inconspicuous yellowish
flowers of the russet buffaloberry (*Shepherdia canadensis*) whose
pistillate and staminate flowers are born on separate plants. Leaves
of arrowleaf balsamroot (*Balsamorhiza sagittata*) are several
inches high, and flower buds are developing. Waterleaf's
(*Hydrophyllum capitatum*) pinnately divided leaves are two to
three inches tall as are the basal, hairy, fern-like leaves of long-
plumed avens (*Geum triflorum*). The first year linear leaves of the
biennial green gentian *(Frasera speciosa)* appear in clusters, now
six to eight inches high. They are snipped off by hungry deer and
elk.

The succulent grass-like leaves of death camas are now heavily
grazed. Learning to recognize these plants at the time of leafing

and budding indicates where to look for them when they flower, as well as when to look for other plants blooming simultaneously. An example might be the bright yellow flower buds of holly-grape (*Mahonia repens*) now slowly opening as death camas leaves enlarge. Wyeth biscuitroot, its yellow umbel of flowers covering patches of disturbed or bare ground, is approaching its peak of flowering as has the inconspicuous Indian potato.

In open spots within the sagebrush habitat, early spring flowers cover patches of ground or extensive areas with their colorful blooms. A few inches below them in the soil lies a fabulous storehouse of readily available food—bulbs and corms of spring beauty, Lewisia *(Lewisia pygmaea)*, Indian potato, shooting star, biscuitroot, and yellowbell. Some of these bulbs (spring beauty) may be an inch in diameter. This starchy food provides sustenance for bears and rodents, even calories for man under emergency conditions. These early flowers will continue to bloom for weeks, appearing later at higher elevations and at the interface of wet soil and late melting snow. The combination of persistent snow-pack and altitude can make a difference of a month from one year to the next in the blooming of early flowering plants, such as spring beauty.

Shooting Star

Pronghorn antelope show up in Grand Teton National Park when aspen, narrow-leaf cottonwood, and some willow catkins are conspicuous. Aspen leaves are just unfolding to give a light green tinge to aspen stands. Leaves of river hawthorn, chokecherry, and snowberry are just appearing as yellow-rumped warblers and white-crowned sparrows start nest building. In a few protected sites wild strawberries and early paintbrush may be in bloom. The first calliope hummingbird may be sighted.

BY THE FIRST WEEK in May, Jackson Hole is usually clear of snow except for lingering cornices and deep drifts, but in some years snow still blankets much of the valley in the vicinity of Moose, Wyoming. When this delayed melting of snow cover occurs, flowering plants are late in appearing and there is considerable variation in time of first bloom from one year to the next. Nevertheless, raven eggs are hatching, and ospreys, sandhill cranes, and red-tailed hawks are incubating. Yellow-headed blackbirds and even comma and red admiral butterflies can be seen against a background of snow. White phlox will now be observed frequently on warm, southeast-facing slopes receiving direct sunlight. Under the lodgepole pine *(Pinus contorta)*, elk sedge (*Carex geyeri)* is flowering. Aspen, narrowleaf cottonwood, and some willow catkins are quite conspicuous with developing aspen leaves providing a warm, yellow-green tinge to wooded slopes. The leaves of shrubs such as currant *(Ribes,* sp*.)*, river hawthorn (*Crataegus rivularis)*, chokecherry (*Prunus melanocarpa)*, and snowberry (*Symphoricarpos oreophilus*) are slowly enlarging.

The green coloring of the vegetation is due to chlorophyll, a pigment that enables the plant, through the process of photosynthesis, to utilize the energy of the sun in manufacturing carbohydrates from water and carbon dioxide while releasing oxygen during daylight hours. Chlorophyll is the most important organic compound on earth. Almost all life forms are directly or indirectly dependent upon chlorophyll for their existence. When young Canada goose goslings hatch or young ground squirrels leave their burrows, the green grass and herbs are present for their immediate consumption. The goslings or squirrels, in turn, may eventually provide a meal for a hungry coyote, badger, mink, or raven. This is the season in the northern hemisphere for the conversion of light energy to chemical energy. The light green coloring of

Aspen Leaves Unfolding

the landscape is a sign of the production and use of new stores of energy for new plant and animal life.

Most Canada geese are still incubating eggs (a twenty-eight-day period); however early

Pronghorn Antelope

hatching goslings may now appear on the scene, along with hatches of the small, olive-gray mayfly—the latter event an indicator of spring to the fly fisher. Trumpeter swans are beginning to build their nest platforms, often on the tops of muskrat lodges. Incubation will begin after completion of egg laying and will last for about thirty-five days. The annual occurrence of animal related events is increasing in tempo, and the appearance of leaves and flowering plants is rapidly altering the landscape. Calliope hummingbirds put in a first appearance as the total number of flowering plants, now including wild strawberries (*Fragaria vesca*) and early paintbrush (*Castilleja chromosa*), furnish an adequate nectar supply. Mountain bluebirds and tree swallows are fighting over nest sites, particularly in aspens. More and more insects become active. Slow moving tiger salamanders appear. Pronghorns show up in the valley having once again completed their spring return trek from desert wintering areas around Pinedale and Farson, Wyoming. Some migrating bull elk will be seen with newly growing antlers in the velvet.

*Canada goose goslings are hatching, trumpeter
swans and American white pelicans are laying eggs
as Yellowstone Lake begins to become ice-free.
Tree swallows are now numerous, some American
dippers are incubating eggs, and mallards are
covering a full clutch of ten or twelve eggs.
The male ruffed grouse courtship drumming
is audible about the time the first blooms of
yellow-flowered groundsel and waterleaf appear.*

MANY DOWNY, yellow, Canada goose goslings will appear on or beside the Snake River about the time you can expect the first appearance of yellow warblers. New grass greens the open meadows, producing food for adult and young geese. The precocious goslings will be out of the nest and swimming a few hours after the last egg in the clutch has hatched. Parents will take their young to grassy meadows to feed, traveling considerable distances overland when necessary. At the time these geese are hatching, canoeists, rafters, and boaters of all kinds should exercise special care to avoid them. A family scattered in swift water will find it difficult to get together again. Having lost track of its mother, a gosling may accept the boat as its foster mother and follow it on downstream. In a short time the raft is imprinted on

Canada Goose Goslings

the gosling as its mother. Trustfully following a "mother raft" is not the ideal way for a gosling to reach adulthood.

When Canada goose goslings are taking to the water, trumpeter swans are finishing nest building and are starting to lay eggs on nest platforms laboriously constructed from stems, leaves, and roots of aquatic vegetation. I watched this process through binoculars from a distance. With her back to me, the female swan stretched out her long neck and with her bill grabbed stems and roots, pulling them back toward her with a swing of her head. This was repeated again and again, each load being dropped back near her tail. Often, this crane-like maneuver was almost too fast for my eye to follow. It was slowed when stubborn stalks or roots caused the swan to put her head deep under water, where

Trumpeter Swan

a steady pull finally loosened the material. After a pile accumulated in the water behind the swan, she swam back and repeated the performance, thus moving the pile of loosened material closer to the platform. She continued this until the nest foundation emerged and more material was placed above water to complete the developing nest. Building may be sped up if the male swan (or cob), joins the female (pen) in the nest-constructing process, but his contributions, while I watched, were almost nil. A raven passing by altered his course to swing in near the nest. The cob was now alert. Perhaps his chief duty was guardian of the nest. The raven would automatically make a note of the incident and store the information for a future use. It could provide him with a meal.

Dark-eyed juncos are now numerous and still in flocks. Brown-headed cowbirds and noisy red-winged blackbirds singing from prominent perches should now be commonly observed. Sharp-shinned hawks are defending territories, though otherwise secretive, preying on the numerous small birds—pine siskins, yellow-rumped warblers, rosy finches, Cassin's finches, mountain bluebirds, American robins, brown-headed cowbirds, Brewer's blackbirds, and a variety of sparrows. Swainson's hawks are still arriving from the south, a bit later than the already well established red-tailed hawks. In an early season, some robins may be incubating eggs, while tree swallows and mountain bluebirds are starting to nest after settling their differences over possession of nest sites in hollow trees or cracks in buildings. Bald and golden eagles have young by now, ospreys and sandhill cranes are incubating eggs—the eagles and osprey in large stick nests, the cranes in a wet area on an elevated mound of reeds, sedges, and cattails.

The nests of some ravens now contain naked young, often a brood of five or six. As the young birds increase in size, space for them in the nest shrinks. Quite often one or more fall or are pushed out of the nest before they have grown their feathers. The parent birds are now foraging seriously and continuously, to satisfy the ravenous appetites. Bird eggs are in good supply. Foraging in pairs, the ravens steal the eggs from Canada geese, herons, and ducks, to mention a few. A little later the ravens will just as effectively and systematically take the helpless young. You may notice, as I often have, that ravens regularly work in concert. I once watched as one engaged the attention of a parent great-blue heron perched on her nest, while another raven, probably not its mate, darted in and picked up an egg in its large black bill and took off before the heron realized she'd been robbed.

Nest of Ravens

On another occasion I watched helpless, shouting in vain, as a raven zeroed in on a straggling gosling, picked it up in its bill, and carried it off. The gosling's legs were flapping futilely, its life span measured in minutes. Through binoculars I watched the legs slow down, then stop. The mortality rate of all young bird nestlings is high, and disturbance by humans or ravens increases it. This raven predation on the young is a natural and nec– essary factor in the control of prey species, rodents as well as geese.

At the same time that the raven is foraging and the heron incubating

Raven

eggs, you may hear a low-pitched throbbing sound. At the start, muffled, it rises in crescendo, the sound usually emanating from the depth of a timbered glade. This low-frequency sound, periodically repeated, is the courtship drumming of the male ruffed grouse, the sound caused by the rapid vibration of the bird's wings held close to the body. The usual stage for this performance is a log, prominently located, yet well concealed. Listen for the first drumming grouse at the peak of blooming of the sagebrush buttercup and spring beauty. It should coincide with the first appearance of the flowers of waterleaf, yellow-flowered groundsel (*Senecio integerrimus*), long-plumed avens, and early paintbrush. At the same time, in coniferous forests, usually at higher altitudes, you may hear the hoot-like calls of the male blue grouse. He displays by spreading his neck feathers to reveal patches of orange-red skin while fanning his tail feathers. Later in the season a distraction display will be used by the blue grouse to lure possible enemies away from precocious, but vul- nerable, young.

When robins are incubating eggs and Canada geese reach their peak of hatching, the first arrowleaf balsamroot and Nelson's larkspur bloom. You can start looking for morels when cottonwoods start to green. Cow moose are giving birth to calves when common snipe are incubating eggs. Ground squirrels are giving birth, young badgers can be seen near den entrances. Calliope hummingbirds are mating. Goshawks are laying eggs, red-tailed hawk eggs are hatching, and mourning cloak butterflies are relatively more numerous.

THE NARROWLEAF cottonwood catkins are usually conspicuous by the time buffaloberry flowers are in full bloom, and Rocky Mountain maple (*Acer glabrum*) leaves are just opening. Gromwell (*Lithospermum incisum*), the first arrowleaf balsamroot and Nelson's larkspur (*Delphinium nelsoni*), and yellow violets are also in bloom. Drooping flowers of mountain bluebell (*Mertensia viridis)* as well as Jacob's ladder *(Polemonium pulcherrimum)* can be expected.

It is a time to look for tasty morel mushrooms—the sponge morel (*Morchella esculenta)* and the earlier black morel (*Morchella angusticeps*). Of the two, the black is a bit earlier and more flavorsome. Morels may or may not be up, depending on temperature and moisture conditions. Walking beneath the cottonwoods in the Snake River bottomlands, you may fill a knapsack or return home empty handed. If unsuccessful on your first mushroom hunt of the season, keep

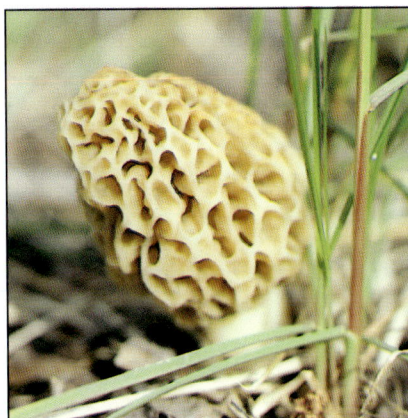

Morel

trying, especially if there has been a change in weather. Being somewhat selective in the area covered increases your chances for success. Start looking under dead but standing cottonwood trees. Next look in the vicinity of fallen cottonwood trunks and limbs. Walk slowly, stopping now and then to completely turn around, scanning the ground close up and at a distance. By changing the direction of your search, morels not visible from one angle will pop into view from another. Take time to thoroughly scan any area where you locate a morel. More may miraculously seem to appear, perhaps a flush of several dozen mushrooms. If you pick more than you can eat at one or two meals, slice the remaining ones and sun-dry for later consumption. Be sure to carefully check your identification. If new at the hobby, eat only a small amount the first time.

Robins are now incubating eggs, and some early nesters have young a few days old. Look for the first western tanagers, easily spotted by the bright yellow, red, and contrasting black of the male. Soon, nesting activities will begin. Yellow and yellow-rumped warblers should now be more numerous.

You may now see lark sparrows, and you should hear the melodious song of the male western meadowlark, directed, at least in part, to his mate incubating eggs in a well-concealed grass nest on the ground.

Elk in small bands, led by an experienced old cow, are still moving northward past Blacktail Butte, on their migration to higher summer ranges. Upon leaving the refuge, some will go to the base of Mt. Leidy, others to Two Ocean Plateau, and some on to Yellowstone National Park. The first destinations will be former calving grounds. At the same time the elk are migrating, some cutthroat trout are moving up small streams that flow into Yellowstone Lake or they are swimming up the Snake River and into tributary streams such as Cottonwood, Polecat, and Blacktail Spring Creek.

Within a few weeks (early June), the cutthroat trout start spawning. In coarse gravel, the female of a pair uses her tail to excavate a saucer-shaped depression (redd) where she deposits her eggs. She is helped by the brightly colored male who excretes milt, the secretion of the male generative organs of fish. As he slaps at her with his tail and body, he is simultaneously dislodging the eggs. Downstream are whitefish feeding on eggs carried to them by the current, overhead are osprey looking for spawning trout, an easy meal. Along the banks are the mink doing likewise. In Yellowstone, grizzlies seek out the small streams flowing into Yellowstone's lakes and gorge themselves on trout. Having once feasted

Cutthroat Trout

at these spawning sites, they will return year after year around the first of June. Most cutthroat spawning will be completed by mid-July. Not all spawning runs will occur at the same time but will be dictated by water temperatures.

Common mergansers may now be seen with young a few weeks old, others a few days old. Sometimes a mother will have fifteen to seventeen young mergansers trailing her, with one or more riding on her back. Later in the year when the young trout have developed, the mergansers will feed on the fry and finger-lings. The number of trout eggs produced (one thousand or more per female) must be great to offset the high mortality.

When touring Yellowstone, it is interesting to compare ob-served phenological events at various locations with those of the base area (Moose, Wyoming). For example, you might drive

Arrowleaf Balsamroot

around Yellowstone National Park on about the third week of May and pull off the Mt. Washburn Highway at the hairpin curve overlook. Here, at an altitude of about 8,000 feet, you might be impressed with your observation that conditions are almost identical to those observed and recorded at Moose, Wyoming, (altitude 6,500 feet) about a month earlier (April 17-23). Here, as earlier at Moose, the aspen catkins are fully out as are the flowers of the sagebrush buttercup, yellowbells, and Wyeth biscuitroot. Mountain bluebirds are checking out possible nesting hollows, and robins have established nesting territories. Yellow-bellied marmots are out of hibernation, but a food supply of green vegetation is still scarce. The similarity between phenological events at the two sites at different times (a month apart) is immediately evident. The difference in altitude between the two sites, (Moose at 6,500 feet, Mount Washburn at 8,000 feet) is 1,500 feet. Applying Hopkins' findings to these events, we get an average of one day later for each 100 feet in altitude, or fifteen days. The difference in latitude between the two sites (Moose at 43.6, Washburn at 44.7) is about one degree north latitude or four days later. This computes to a total of nineteen days later for the same events to occur on Mt. Washburn. The difference in time between the recorded events and the computed ones is a result of a number of influencing variables. Sometimes these can be determined or even measured. Regardless of the degree of variation in the timing of predicted events, as opposed to observed events, a great deal can be learned about the effects of weather, altitude, climate, and local factors that influence plant growth and development. Their influence on concurrent animal activities may also be revealed.

*The large yellow flowers of balsamroot are
becoming conspicuous, and extensive fields of solid
golden dandelions are approaching peak of
blooming. Yellow flowers definitely monopolize the
scene with yellow violets also at or near their peak.
Kestrels and great gray owls are laying their eggs.
Long-eared owls, snipe, and killdeer are
incubating eggs, and bull elk are sporting
well-developed antlers in the velvet.*

MALE RUFFED GROUSE are regularly and frequently drumming when balsamroot first blooms. Common snipe fill the air
with the sound of their courtship dives. Yellow warblers are nest
building, and male house wrens are exploring nesting hollows
and filling some with sticks—the female may take her choice.
Great horned owls with young can be heard hooting from the
vicinity of their nests, while a new sound, the call of the chorus
frogs, emanates from wet, marshy areas. Great gray owls are
starting to incubate their eggs. Their time of laying varies consid-
erably, perhaps influenced by availability of suitable nest sites.
Old goshawk nests are often used but are not plentiful. Chipping
sparrows are nest building, common snipe and killdeer are incubating eggs, and some kestrels have a full clutch of five eggs that

will hatch in about twenty-eight days. Barn swallows appear, tree swallows are feeding young, a first of two broods, and cliff swallows are busy building their mud nests. Cowbirds appear, joining mixed flocks of red-winged blackbirds, yellow-headed blackbirds, Brewer's blackbirds, common grackles, and starlings.

As the days continue to lengthen and day and night temperatures become warmer, more and more flowers bloom; the total number as well as the number of flowering species increases. The evergreen leaves of snowbrush (*Ceanothus velutinus*) emerge from hard-packed snowbanks or cornices and, soon after, clumps of white flowers appear. Valerian, or tobacco root, (*Valeriana dioica*) and long-leaved phlox (*Phlox longifolia*) approach their peak of flowering but continue blooming clear into the fall. The drooping purple flowers of sugarbowl (*Clematis hirsutissima*) are just appearing, the delicate star flowers are about finished blooming, and the male flowers of elk sedge are giving off pollen. The correlation of animal activities and plant blooming and leafing is more accurate as an indicator of events

Great Gray Owl

Yellow Warbler's Nest

when the time of first appearances is used. At other times the peak of blooming is more meaningful and helpful.

When the balsamroot first blooms, look for the first puffballs (*Calvatia*). Depending on the species and on local growing conditions, they may be the size of a quarter or as big around as a child's head. The first time I found puffballs of this large a size my excitement must have been transmitted to my young children who were with me. To this day, as adults, they are excited by such a find. Puffballs, when sliced with a knife, will show a uniform white consistency within the outer shell—no gills present. If doubtful, don't eat them. If sure, slice them into sections, fry in butter, and enjoy an exotic addition to your meal. Sun-dry the surplus for later consumption.

At this time, when the white-flowered death camas, poisonous to man and stock, is just blooming, you may look for the first appearance of yellow swallowtail butterflies and cecropia moths. You will

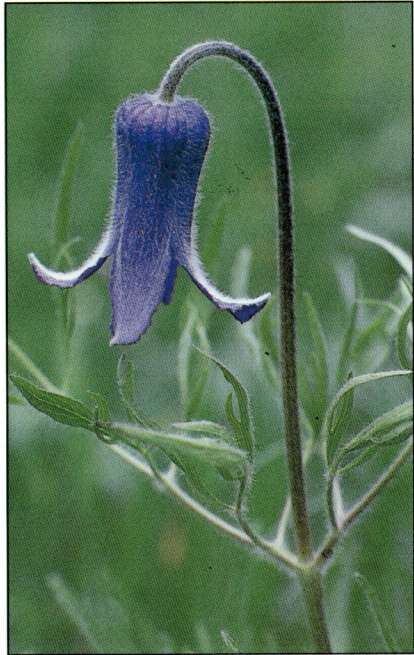

Sugarbowl

MICHAEL S. SAMPLE

find Sheridan's hairstreak butterflies in the sagebrush among the buckwheat plants. When the weather is favorable, and depending on the year, you may see hundreds, if not thousands, of painted-lady butterflies flitting over the landscape as they emerge from hibernation. By now, mourning cloak butterflies will be relatively common. They seem to be attracted to sap oozing from insect bore holes in aspens and cottonwoods.

In late spring and early summer, two-grooved milkvetch (*Astragalus bisulcatus*) and locoweed (*Oxytropis* sp.) appear, as well as the crazyweeds (*Oxytropis bessyi*). The keel or lower petals of *Oxytropis* are abruptly contracted into a distinct beak. The keel of *Astragalus* flowers is not beaked. Many plants of these two genera are poisonous to animals and man, but it is not easy to distinguish between those that are and those that are not poisonous. The tall growing, purple-flowered, two-grooved milkvetch produces a fruit pod having two parallel rounded grooves. It is one of the local poisonous species. These plants are able to absorb large quantities of minerals such as selenium and molybdenum, both of which are poisonous in relatively small quantities to man and other animals. Many species of this pea family, *Leguminosae*, are edible, but others poisonous. Check your identification carefully before eating.

*The runoff flow of the Snake River peaks, creating
ideal conditions for white-water boating, both
private and commercial. By early June, female
pronghorns, soon to give birth, have enlarged
bellies. Coyote pups are out of the den. Cow elk
and mule deer are dropping a few early calves.
Yellow fields of dandelions have turned white, and
pine siskins are busy feeding on the limitless supply
of tufted seeds. The first white blooms of
serviceberry are appearing when sandhill crane
eggs are hatching. Harlequin ducks have now
arrived, and some young ravens and great horned
owls are fledging.*

WHEN ENTIRE FIELDS are white with the seed heads of
dandelions, many species of birds that have been quietly incubating eggs become hyperactive feeding young. Among these are
robins, mountain bluebirds, starlings, crows, ravens, great horned
owls, red-tailed hawks, sandhill cranes, and great blue herons.
Aspen leaves have turned a darker hue, but cottonwoods still
exhibit a light green color. The first white flowers of serviceberry
(*Amelanchier alnifolia*) appear, Wyeth biscuitroot reaches its
peak of flowering, and holly-grape is in full bloom. Red twinberry

(Lonicera utahensis), fairybells *(Disporum trachycarpum)*, sugarbowl, and bluebonnet lupine *(Lupinus sericeus)* are also in bloom.

House wrens, flickers, downy and hairy woodpeckers, red-naped sapsuckers, juncos, ruffed grouse, long-billed curlews, ospreys, and calliope hummingbirds are now nesting; the latter are diving at or literally "dive-bombing" intruders—other hummingbirds as well as humans. Where this defense occurs, look for a nearby nest, but don't feel discouraged if you don't find it. The nest is tiny and well concealed. The eggs of the hummingbird take fourteen to sixteen days to hatch, those of the osprey and trumpeter swan about thirty-three to thirty-seven days. Incubation in these cases is by the female alone. Generally speaking, the larger the bird and the egg, the longer it takes the egg to hatch (Table VIII).

JANA C. SMITH

Bluebonnet Lupine, Geranium

Many of the berry producing plants that will provide food for wildlife in the fall are now in bloom. This includes serviceberry, buffaloberry, black and golden currant (*Ribes lacustre* and *aureum*), holly-grape, chokecherry, red twinberry and black twinberry (*Lonicera involucrata*), elderberry (*Sambucus coerulea*), big whortleberry (huckleberry) (*Vaccinium membranaceum*), and grouse whortleberry (*Vaccinium scoparium*). The white-flow-ered racemes of baneberries (*Actaea arguta*) bloom at this time. Later these will develop into attractive glossy red, pink, or white berries. Take note of

Baneberry Flower

this plant in flower and learn its characteristics, for the berries developing from these flowers are poisonous and should not be eaten.

When glacier lilies (*Erythronium grandiflorum*) are still bloom-ing where snow drifts are still melting, when yellow and blue violets *(Viola adunca)* are flowering, and when the white flow-ers of strawberry and the purple flowers of shooting star are in bloom, you may hear the chorus frogs singing, see spawning cutthroat trout and, if lucky, observe the courtship of grizzlies. It is the beginning of the June mating season and a time of year when the large male grizzlies and the relatively smaller females are regularly seen together.

At this time when nestling golden eagles are a few weeks old, a number of conspicuous shrubs are in bloom. All are found within the hunting ranges and nesting areas of golden eagles. Annually, buffaloberry appear first, followed in sequence by serviceberry, bitterbrush, chokecherry, and hawthorn. All may be in bloom at the same time, but with buffaloberry fading out as the hawthorn is just beginning to flower. When these plants are blooming, the nesting cycle of the golden eagle is well underway in the Greater Yellowstone Ecosystem. Look for parent eagles carrying food to the nests. Some five hundred miles farther south at the 6,000 foot level around Kanab, Utah, the flowering sequence of serviceberry, bitterbrush, and chokecherry is similar to that at Moose, but has occurred earlier by about five or six weeks.

The recorded fledging of golden eagles has occurred about one month earlier at Kanab. The use of plant indicators to help to determine when to look for nesting activities of certain birds, such as the golden eagle, can be useful when planning birding or photography trips to the peripheries of the ecosystem or even beyond.

Young Golden Eagle

*Young coyotes are just emerging from their dens
when the light yellow flowers of bitterbrush are
giving a yellow cast to large areas of sagebrush.
The scattered white flower clusters of serviceberry
are approaching their peak of flowering as are the
inconspicuous flowers of the rusty menziesia and
huckleberries—big whortleberries and grouse
whortleberries. Trumpeter swans and northern
goshawks are incubating eggs. Young bluebirds are
feathering, and blue flax, silky phacelia, and
golden corydalis are making their first appearance.*

ABOUT THE TIME that yellow-flowered groundsel and sugar
bowl are at peak of flowering, Nelson's larkspur is becoming
more and more prominent. The harlequin ducks begin nesting
along the fast-water stretches of the Snake River and its tributaries. They have completed an annual flight from the coast of the
Pacific Ocean where they winter to the streams of the Greater
Yellowstone area where they nest in hollow trees or piles of river
driftwood. The strikingly-colored male stays only long enough to
establish a territory and mate before returning to the west coast.
The drab-colored female is left alone to care for her rambunctious
young that seem to exude happiness as they swim, frolic, and

Coyote

feed in white water that appears tempestuous enough to drown them. All, however, is not pleasure, as evidenced by the decrease in the size of the broods from day to day. When very young, they may make a tasty meal for a hungry California gull.

When the mountain suckers are moving upstream to spawn in waters of about fifty degrees, they are sometimes so densely packed as to obscure the stream bottom. Look for the suckers when mallard ducks and common mergansers have young a few days to a week old. Cinnamon teals, green-winged teals, American wigeons, and wood ducks are nesting; mature Canada geese are starting to molt their flight feathers; and snipe and osprey are incubating eggs. Long-billed curlews are usually heard before they are seen vigorously defending their nests from maurading ravens. Chipping sparrows, dark-eyed juncos, and green-tailed towhees are nesting. Western tanagers and lazuli buntings are often visable along with the tiger swallowtails and Glover's silk moths. When the first blue camas (*Camassia quamash*), mules-ears (*Wyethia amplexicaulis*), and sticky geranium (*Geranium visco-sissimum*) appear, look for the nests of green-tailed towhees and sparrows such as white-crowned, sage, lark, and chipping. Also making their first appearance at

Blue Flax

this time are rusty menziesia (*Menziesia ferruginea*), blue flax (*Linum lewisii*), silky phacelia (*Phacelia sericea*), and golden corydalis (*Corydalis aurea*). You will probably come across tent caterpillars defoliating chokecherry and bitterbrush bushes.

Swallowtail Butterfly

Blue Camas

Chokecherry, with its slowly opening raceme of white flowers, is just beginning to bloom, as is the river or western black hawthorn. Both will develop dark-bluish fruits over summer that are avidly sought by birds and other forms of wildlife. Both make excellent jelly and pancake syrup but cannot compare in flavor to that of the huckleberries. When fully ripe, the round "apples" of hawthorn (*Crataegus rivularis*) are tasty to munch on in late summer and early fall. The single-seeded choke or frost cherries ripen much later. They can be eaten raw, but don't break open or swallow the contents of the pits. They contain the poison cyanide, which can be eliminated by cooking.

Sandhill crane eggs are hatching, and downy, rusty-brown young are appearing beside the long-legged parents. Tree swallows, downy woodpeckers, and mountain bluebirds are feeding their young still in nesting hollows. A few tree swallows are doing the same with offspring that have just fledged. Calliope hummingbirds are still incubating. Scarlet gilia, Indian paintbrush, elk thistle, and cow parsnip are beginning to bloom as lodgepole pines sporadically fill the air with drifting clouds of yellow pollen. Lake fishing is good, but mosquitoes along shorelines are becoming more aggravating. This at the same time pink-flowered swamp-laurel is in bloom.

WHILE MOTHER Barrow's goldeneyes herd their week-old broods of young through reflections on the placid waters of beaver ponds, adult killdeer are feigning wounded bird acts to lure observers and predators away from their precocious young. These killdeer young are just out of the eggs, yet able to hide by remaining motionless or to evade danger by scooting around like moving blobs of sunlight.

The yellow flowers of stonecrop (*Sedum stenopetalum*) have

reached full bloom after a slow process of opening up. On favorable growing sites, such as fields, meadows, and roadsides, the first light yellow flowers of oysterplant (*Tragopogon pratensis*) show up and quickly turn into conspicuous white seed heads that are more enduring and more attractive than the flowers. Viewing these with back lighting enhances the beauty of the fruiting body.

Though the single flowers are fleeting, the flowering season is long and continuous. Flowers now at their peak and giving changing patterns of color to the landscape are balsamroot, mules-ears, snowberry, buckwheat (*Eriogonum heracleoides*), bitterbrush, serviceberry, long-leaved phlox, Nelson's larkspur, and Wyeth biscuitroot. Yellow-flowered groundsel is about finished flowering, but of course can still be seen in full bloom at a higher elevation. In cool, moist years, the peak of blooming for most early flowers is extended. In warm, dry springs, such as in 1988,

Oysterplant

Sandhill Crane

the flowers bloom earlier and fade away much more quickly. The sequence of events remains approximately the same, but the interval between them is shortened. Some flowers making a first appearance that you might look for include twisted-stalk (*Streptopus amplexifolius*), fairyslipper (*Calypso bulbosa*), white bog-orchid (*Habenaria dilatata*), western meadow rue

Elk Thistle

(*Thalictrum occidentale*), spotted coralroot (*Corallorhiza maculata*), lodgepole lupine (*Lupinus parviflorus*), Dyer's woad (*Isatis tinctoria*), anemone (*Anemone globosa*), blue flax, shrubby cinquefoil (*Pentaphylloides floribunda*), silverweed cinquefoil (*Potentilla anserina*), showy cinquefoil (*Potentilla gracilis*), scarlet gilia (*Gilia aggregata*), Indian paintbrush (*Castilleja miniata*), elk thistle (*Cirsium scariosum*), and pink-flowered swamp-laurel (*Kalmia polifolia*).

Barn swallows and cliff swallows are just building nests or incubating eggs when some robins have fledged. Some kestrels are still incubating eggs, usually in hollows that they return to year after year. Cinnamon teals have young a week to ten days old and share the same ponds with the goldeneyes and green-winged teals.

Half-grown ground squirrels, the size of least chipmunks, pop out of their burrows and stand sentinel-like before scampering around. At this stage of development they are particularly vulnerable to coyotes who seek them out and swallow them after only a chew or two—hardly enough, it would seem, to get a proper taste.

Some day-old moose calves are taking their first tottering steps under the surveillance of a protective mother who, under these conditions, will not hesitate to attack. Give them a wide berth, for an aroused mother moose can be as lethal as a grizzly.

Cow Moose and Calf

MICHAEL S. SAMPLE

*Pronghorn mothers are now giving birth to or
nursing young. The flowers of yellow-flowered
groundsel bow out to the yellow flowers of
hawksbeard at about the time of the summer
solstice (June 21), the longest day of the year.
Below freezing temperatures are still possible.
Mountain death camas fades, yampa and columbine
appear as some cliff swallows are building nests.
White-crowned sparrows are feeding young,
and horned owl fledglings can be heard calling to
their parents for food when goshawks' eggs
are just hatching.*

BY THE TIME of the summer solstice, all of the deciduous
trees and shrubs are about fully leafed out, making locating of
nests and observation of nesting birds more difficult than earlier
in the season. Under such conditions, the goshawks may remain
silent as you approach their nest. But once they recognize that the
nest has been discovered, both adults, particularly the female,
will put up a defense of the young expressed in noisy cackling
and diving at the intruder. Red eyes seem to expand as they flash
by, inches from your face. If, in the course of a raptor study, you
climb a tree in order to determine whether the nest contains eggs

Young Antelope

or young and how many or to weigh, measure, and photograph them, you should be prepared for an all-out aggressive attack, and to protect your face, eyes, and body from contact with the hawk's raking talons. This also applies should you take an eyas for falconry purposes from a nest on non-park land. A permit is required for either activity. I have yet to climb to a goshawk nest and not be savagely attacked. On one occasion, the larger female struck me in the back so violently that the impact not only jarred me, but so stunned the hawk that she dropped to the ground in a daze. On another occasion, a similar attack left me with a ripped flannel shirt and a bleeding slash on my back. A hard hat should be standard apparel if you contemplate climbing

71

to a goshawk nest. It is well to remember that, under the right conditions, most raptors will attack and strike a person. To my knowledge, this fortunately does not apply to the largest raptors, the bald and golden eagles.

Though stonefly hatches delight the angler, deer flies and buffalo gnats do not. They now appear to make life miserable for hikers, campers, and anglers. When you sit down to change flies or to adjust a backpack, the sneaky buffalo gnats may quietly move from the grass to your sock band, waist, or neck. Here they anesthetize the skin as they bite. Hours later chigger-like welts appear that spread into a large area of inflammation. The itch alone will assure that you do not forget the white-socks, as they are sometimes called. Insect repellent applied in advance is the best protection, should the presence of insects be noted or suspected.

White-crowned Sparrow

The white compound umbels of yampa (*Perideridia gairdneri*) are now appearing as are the light blue tubular flowers of wild hyacinth (*Triteleia grandiflora*). Yampa has a small, sweet-potato shaped tuber with a parsnip flavor, while wild hyacinth has solid bulbs or corms. Blue camas is at peak of blooming and has edible bulbs, layered

Columbine

like the nodding or wild onion (*Allium cernuum*), also now in bloom. All are excellent wild foods, both for man and wildlife, and are sought out by grizzly bears who routinely visit patches of these plant foods at the same time year after year. (It is this habit, when applied to food obtained in campgrounds and developed areas, that makes potentially dangerous, man-conditioned grizzlies.) Look for these flowers when yellow warblers, western meadowlarks, and calliope hummingbirds are incubating eggs.

Dark-eyed junco eggs are hatching, and cliff and bank swallows are nesting when young starlings and cowbirds are getting together in flocks. White-crowned sparrows, Brewer's blackbirds, pine siskins, and hairy woodpeckers are feeding young and are being harassed by ravens, who see the young of all the nesting birds as sustenance for their hungry offspring. In turn, the red-winged and Brewer's blackbirds dive at and chase the ravens from their nesting territories.

While the above events are taking place, the first flowers of wild rose (*Rosa woodsii*), silverberry *(Eleagnus commutata)*, red-osier dogwood (*Cornus stolonifera*), water parsnip (*Sium suave*), columbine (*Aquilegia coerulea*), and mountain hollyhock (*Iliamna rivularis*) are appearing. The new shoots and maple-shaped leaves of mountain hol-lyhock are a favorite browse of mule deer who locate this plant beside trails, brooks, roadside shoulders, and burned-over forest areas. Hawksbeard (*Crepis acuminata*) is now the dominant yellow flower, and mountain death camas begins to fade. Chokecherry, with its long white racemes, is at the peak of flowering. Numerous blossoms do not necessarily signify a later bounty crop of cherries. Some strawberries are ripe, while others are still in flower. Squawbush (*Rhus trilobata*) berries are small and green.

Common Snipe

Late spawning cutthroat trout are fashioning their redds in the gravel bottom of Blacktail-Spring Creek. Overhead, snipe make their winnowing dives or cackle as they give warning to their young.

*When the white tufted seeds of hawksbeard and the
flowers of western polemonium appear, young
red-tailed hawks and nestling prairie falcons are
in the feathering out stage of development, during
which they continue to gain in weight and size.
The towering stalks of green gentian are in full
bloom as are the white wyethia and mules-ears.
Great gray owl and kestrel eggs are hatching, and
butterflies, moths, and dragonflies are active and
numerous. Watch for the appearance
of salmon flies.*

ELK, DEER, MOOSE, bison, and pronghorn antelope are now less secretive and can be more readily observed with their young. The elk and bison are seeking grasses, sedges, and herbs; the moose, deer, and pronghorns favor the browse plants. The old, shaggy winter coats have been shed and replaced by slick, shiny pelage—the elk a deep brown, the moose almost black, the mule deer a reddish brown.

Nestling great blue herons are about half grown. A parent is usually standing watch nearby ready to protect them from maurading ravens. The nestlings are rapidly approaching the stage where they can defend themselves with their dagger-like

Blue Grouse

bills. Spotted sandpipers and yellow warblers are incubating eggs. Juvenile mountain bluebirds and house wrens are leaving their nest hollows, and pine siskins are fledging. Young blue grouse a week old are keeping close to their mother while the pompous male diverts attention from the scampering brood. Fast growing, young Barrow's goldeneyes are trailing their mothers single file on beaver ponds, having left their hollow tree nests several weeks earlier for wetter and more open spaces.

With the yellow flowers of balsamroot no longer dominant, the now more conspicuous little sunflower (*Helianthella uniflora*) takes its place in the color scheme, being enhanced by the yellow shrubby cinquefoil (*Potentilla fruticosa*), sulphur cinquefoil (*Potentilla recta*), and another yellow cinquefoil, silverweed. Western Polemonium (*Polemonium occidentale*) appear as the white wyethia (*Wyethia helianthoides*) are in full bloom.

Young tree swallows congregate in groups on wires and limbs waiting to be fed by their insect-foraging parents. Hatches of stone flies, caddis flies, crane flies, and mayflies now more frequently inform the fly fisher of the dry fly to use.

The green berries of wild currant, holly-grape, buffaloberry, serviceberry, black twinberry, elderberry, red-osier dogwood, and river hawthorn are all rapidly developing. The white flowers of thimbleberry (*Rubus parviflorus*) and wild red raspberry (*Rubus idaeus*) are just appearing. A few wild strawberries are ripe, but they're usually scarce compared to the number of flowers observed earlier.

With the advent of summer, the orderly progression of blooming from year to year becomes more in sync with the flowering times of previous years. There is now less influence from weather variables such as snow depth, snow persistence, storms, chilly or freezing nights, extended periods of rain, overcast skies, or drought. Summer has arrived, and it is evident in the profusion and diversity of flowers and the varied nesting activities of a large number of bird species ranging from Calliope hummingbirds to golden eagles.

Young ground squirrels, meadow mice, chipmunks, pocket gophers, and yellow-bellied marmots are being picked off by

Young Red Fox

coyotes, badgers, and red foxes—all with young to feed. They are taking their toll of the annual increase in the rodent populations. The mammalian predators are competing with the raptors for the same prey species, yet at the same time automatically collaborating in the reduction and control of rodents, species whose productivity is geared to compensate for such losses.

When the yellow clouds of lodgepole pollen are being whisked across the tree tops and are building up in yellow masses along the lakeshores, look for other but quite different clouds. These clouds are composed of hundreds of thousands of large-bodied salmon flies, largest of all the stoneflies, with wingspreads of three to four inches. They are called salmon flies because they are a beautiful salmon pink color. Emergence occurs at different times and throughout a number of days. It is largely influenced by warming water and by elevation, the flies appearing when water temperatures reach fifty degrees or more. Hatches occur in

Salmon Fly

canyons or along vegetated stream banks and rocky shorelines. Here the nymphal form lives under rocks and debris in fast, well-aerated water. First emergence occurs down-stream and moves up as the water temperature rises. In late spring or early summer when the flowers of yellow sweet clover (*Melilotus officinalis)* first appear along highway shoulders, when little sunflower and blue flax are blooming, the salmon fly nymphs leave the water and crawl about on shore, where they cling to rocks, trees, and other vegetation. Here they shed their nymphal husks (shucks) and unfold and dry their wings prior to flying. Soon after they are airborne, the females fly low, dipping their abdomens in the water while depositing eggs in the stream.

In some areas, such as the Canyon of the Yellowstone River, I have observed late morning hatches that looked like locust hordes, the sky seething with the moving insects. Circling birds first indicated the presence of a hatch. Ravens and California gulls cut swaths through the moving mass as they fed voraciously on the insects. Trout gorged themselves on the limitless food supply and put on layers of fat that serve them well in leaner days ahead. I looked on, too entranced to feel disappointment at the trout's lack of interest in my artificial flies. This is an amazing spectacle, one that can provide a fly fisher enjoyment and satisfaction even if nary a trout is hooked.

Flowers are diverse and abundant, coloring the landscape and microhabitats. When the flower heads of the golden-colored foxtail barley line highway shoulders, you will also see the flowers of yellow sweet clover. With the peaking of scarlet gilia or blue penstemon, you can expect to see many species of young birds in the nest or just leaving it—black-headed grosbeaks, house wrens, American robins, tree swallows, mountain bluebirds, white-crowned sparrows, red-winged blackbirds, yellow warblers, prairie falcons, and long-eared owls. Female calliope hummingbirds are incubating eggs, the males defending territories. Cooper's hawks' eggs are hatching. Some 150 species of birds are now involved in some stage of nesting activities (Table II).

THE ELDERBERRY and mountain ash (*Sorbus scopulina*) flowers bloom, along with little sunflower and houndstongue (*Cynoglossum officinale*). To distinguish between elderberry and mountain ash, the former has opposite compound leaves; the latter, alternate.

First appearing in mid-June, the blue flax is now conspicuous.

Young Prairie Falcon

The flowers close up at night and open in the morning with the increase of heat and light. The open flowers face the sun, the leaning stems straining to track it across the sky. The oysterplant does the same, forming a spectacular yellow blanket when the yellow blooms in a large patch all face in the same direction. Golden asters (*Heterotheca villosa*), yellow stonecrop, yellow sweet clover, and little sunflower add more yellow to the wildflower gardens.

With one or more of these flowers as a background, yellow warblers flit back and forth among the willows, cautiously approaching their nest to feed their young. At times it is difficult to distinguish between the rapid movements of these birds and the reflection of sunlight off an early yellowing willow leaf moving in the wind. The female yellow warblers complete their rapid nest building with the appearance of the blue flax and the oysterplant, and the young warblers may fledge when stonecrop flowers are at peak of blooming. Foxtail barley (*Hordeum jubatum*) and blue penstemon (*Penstemon cyaneus*) are also at their peak.

Musk or bristle thistle (*Carduus nutans*) is just appearing, and grasses are filling the air with pollens, causing discomfort to those allergic or sensitive to them. At the same time, the fluff-bearing seeds from the willows, and narrowleaf and broadleaf cottonwoods float through the air or lodge in cottony masses where trapped in niches and crevices. They, too, can cause breathing discomfort or hay fever. In the river bottoms, where large diameter cottonwoods in the course of succession are being replaced by spruce or fir, you may witness a fascinating, though common, event—a full-blown blizzard in early July. A light breeze ruffles the cottonwood leaves and seed pods, causing an outpouring of drifting cotton. With wind increasing the cottony storm, the white falling "snow" outlined against the dark background of

Cottonwood Fluff and Seeds

spruce trees is indeed a replica of a winter blizzard, so real that you may reach for your hood before realizing it is summer.

When the scarlet gilia and Indian paintbrush, the Wyoming state flower, are adding their red colors to the scene, the rufous hummingbirds arrive. They appear within a few days of their arrival time in past years. The calliope and broad-tailed hummingbirds are already nesting. Hummingbirds seem to prefer getting their nectar from red flowers. Early in the season, scarlet gilia produces brilliant red blooms to entice its hummingbird

MICHAEL S. SAMPLE

East Rosebud River

pollinators. But, according to Ken Paige, in the Fern Mountain area of Arizona, the flowers change to a white color in fall, possibly an adaptation to the emigration of the hummingbirds. The white flowers are preferred by hawkmoths that continue the pollination after the hummers leave.

84

When you see the red-purplish flowers of elephant-head, the full flowering of the white bog-orchid, and the opening blossoms of mountain hollyhocks, you can expect to find a few adult Canada geese, still flightless, but their molting nearly complete. Young bald eagles are leaving their nest as are also some kestrels and young great gray owls. Young Swainson's hawks are still growing feathers to replace down as are the ospreys. Sharp-shinned hawk eggs are just hatching. Most cutthroat trout spawning is completed.

THE SEASON has now reached a stage where the maximum number of flower species are blooming, some plants sparingly, such as the orchids, ladies tresses *(Spiranthes romanzoffiana)*, and fairyslippers. Others, such as elk thistle, cow parsnip, snowberry, bluebonnet, and sticky geranium bloom in profusion. Some of these flowers that you may now expect to see are listed at the end of this weekly sequence.

Young Uinta ground squirrels and least chipmunks, nearly half-grown, are scooting around in their sagebrush-grass habitat. Cliff swallows are fledging; young sage grouse have grown to about the size of bobwhite quail. Young ruffed grouse in river bottom thickets are half grown but are still diligently herded about by a protective mother. Young birds and also young rodents, such as the least chipmunks, meadow mice, white-footed mice, yellow-bellied marmots, and red squirrels, are becoming more

Marmot

JANA C. SMITH

abundant for predators, including the adult and young of the long-eared owl. By collecting and analyzing pellets from under nests and roosting perches, one can obtain a representation of the raptor diet. Insects, now more prevalent and diverse, are food for fledging barn swallows and other passerine birds. Nesting common nighthawks are efficiently scooping up insects in their erratic flight. Golden stoneflies are hatching out, giving the fly fisher a pleasure and a clue to the dry fly to select. Feeding birds, such as western kingbirds, willow flycatchers, robins, and even red-naped sapsuckers, when seen darting above the bushes and out over the streams, indicate where you may find rising trout. As you plod over the shoreline gravel bars, you should see colorful patches of lavender broadleaf fireweed (*Epilobium latifolium*).

Rocky Mountain pine bark beetles can be heard clicking in the lodgepole pines in galleries beneath the bark. These beetles have in the recent past killed large numbers of lodgepole pine trees. These losses may in some areas hasten the succession to whitebark pine. The brownish moths of the spruce budworm are visible flitting from branch

Dwarf Fireweed

87

Elephanthead

to branch of the Douglas fir and subalpine fir (*Abies lasiocarpa),* which their larvae eventually kill by defoliating the trees year after year. The death of many of these trees, two to three hundred years old, as well as the loss of the mature but younger pines, greatly alters the plant communities as well as the overall environment. Goshawks, for example, find former nesting and hunting territories unsuitable. In turn, the great gray owl that usurps the old goshawk nests, must look elsewhere. Red squirrels move out of the dead forests, many species of woodpeckers move in, and downed timber blocks game trails and re-routes ungulate travel. The steady accumulation of tinder, along with efficient fire suppression, sets the stage for conflagrations, similar to the Yellowstone fires of 1988.

Fires of this intensity and magnitude drastically alter the existing state of plant succession. A climax spruce-fir forest, with its plant and animal communities that have evolved over hundreds of years, can be literally wiped out in a matter of hours. The whole regenerative process begins again, starting from crustose lichens on rock where the heat was intense, to areas of lesser heat where grasses, herbaceous plants, shrubs, subclimax and climax species succeed one another. Each successional stage flourishes and makes growing conditions favorable for the next community of plants. The early and intermediate stages of plant succession will provide a greater diversity of plant foods for ungulates, bears, and other wildlife. This is one objective of the policy to let naturally-caused fires burn in areas where it has been predetermined that burning would be beneficial. But taking the position that lightning-caused fires

Young Fireweed Plant

should be permitted to die out naturally when fire hazard is high, is unrealistic.

The Yellowstone landscape for years to come will consist of blackened tree spires. On the other hand, the scorched ground will be covered with green vegetation in a few years. Some of the first plant invaders to appear following the fire will be grasses, fireweed (*Epilobium angustifolium*), spirea (*Spiraea splendens*), grouse whortleberry, dogbane (*Apocynum androsaemifolium*), snowbrush, lupine (*Lupinus perennis*), and arnica (*Arnica cordifolia*), along with seedling lodgepole pines whose cones are opened by fire and whose seeds are dispersed by the wind. From underground runners, aspen will send up a profusion of shoots.

If you hike the Taggart Lake Trail in Grand Teton National Park, you can see the vegetation and some of the animal species that have appeared to soften the scar of the 1985 Beaver Creek (or Taggart Lake) fire. Across the valley from this burn is the 1988 Shadow Mountain or Hunter burn. It is accessible by car. Here you can compare the new vegetation on a burned area with that of a lightly or unburned area.

In the sage-grass habitats, white and pink snowberry flowers, though not conspicuous, are abundant and widespread. The round white berries will appear later. The green fruits of the red rasp-berries, the developing berries of elderberry, silverberry, thimble-berry, serviceberry, gooseberry *(Ribes* sp.*)*, currants, and red twinberry are in various stages of growth. The fruits of chokecher-ries and red-osier dogwood are just beginning to develop. The berries of red-osier are not edible, but the reddish bark mixed with the dry ground leaves of bearberry (or kinnikinnick) (*Arctostaphylos uva-ursi*) was smoked as a tobacco substitute by the Indians. The red mealy fruits of bearberry are edible but not particularly appealing. The chokecherry will be one of the last berries to ripen—but not until after several fall frosts.

The chokecherry crop varies from year to year, ranging from almost no cherries, to autumns when branches are bent under the weight of the fruit. At other times the chokecherry midge gall, a fly-like insect, infests developing fruit. Its larvae hatch from the midge eggs and burrow into the pit of the cherry, thus distorting the fruit and making it unfit for berry gatherers.

JANA C. SMITH

Lupine, Geranium, Paintbrush

The overall seasonal peak of flowering occurs at about this time, July 10 - 16. Some of the flowers in bloom, from first flowering to peak and decline, are:

alfalfa	pink spirea
ballhead sandwort	red monkeyflower
bedstraw	scarlet gilia
bluebonnet lupine	sego lily
blue flax	showy daisy
bristle (or musk) thistle	sticky geranium
butter-and-eggs	sweet vetch
Canada thistle	tall larkspur
cinquefoil or five fingers	thickstem aster
cow parsnip	water buttercup
elephanthead	water parsnip
elk thistle	western coneflower
fairyslipper	white bog-orchid
false dandelion	white spirea
fernleaf	wild strawberry
fever few	woolly yellow daisy
foxtail	yarrow
golden aster	yellow pondlily
goldenrod	
harebell	***Some developing berries and fruits are:***
Indian paintbrush	arnica cordifolia seeds
ladies tresses	buffaloberries
little sunflower	curlydock seeds
loveroot	golden currants
monkshood	huckleberries
mountain bluebell	leopard lily pods
mountain hollyhock	mountain ash berries
ox-eye daisy	nettle seeds
oysterplant	silverberries
parrots-beak	twinberry honeysuckle
pink pyrola	whortleberries

Some adult Canada geese are still flightless, not yet having completed their annual molt, and some adult Uinta ground squirrels are ready to hibernate. These events occur about the time fireweed and goldenrod are in full bloom. Young tree swallows are gathering in flocks, young ravens are feeding themselves, filling up on grasshoppers, and goshawks are fledging. Bald eagles have already fledged, young osprey are well feathered and about to leave the nest. Elk thistle reaches its peak of flowering, and bristle thistle reveals its flowers and thorns.

FROM THE TIME of the summer solstice (June 21), the longest day of the year, until a month later, the flowering of plants and the reproduction of most animals have reached a collective peak. Many flowering plants blooming earlier have faded away or have become conspicuous in fruit, plants such as sugarbowl and white clematis (or virgin's bower) (*Clematis ligusticifolia),* with their tufted seeds, or the edible but less conspicuous pods of the glacier lily. Alfalfa is blooming and yampa flowers, with their umbels of small white blossoms, are more in evidence. Canada thistle and bristle thistle are in bloom. The showy daisy, bedstraw, tall

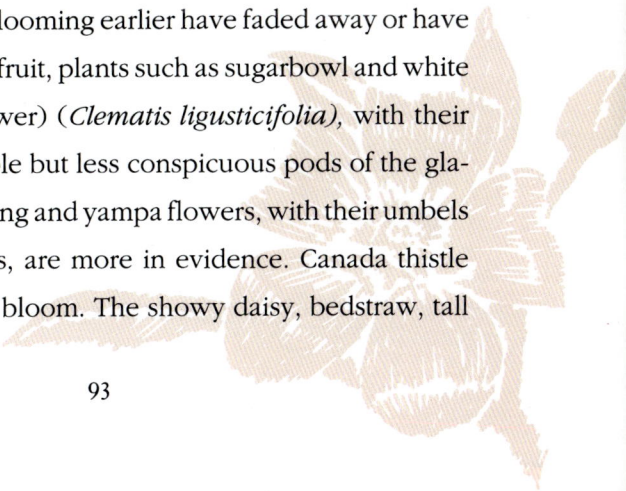

larkspur, cow parsnip, water parsnip, and harebell are now at their peak of flowering.

Young sandhill cranes, half grown, can be seen feeding with their parents in meadows or wet areas. This is a contrast in habitat from the fast moving rivers and streams where the common merganser feeds on fish and leads a large family of half- to three-quarter-grown ducklings across swirling currents to a safe harbor. When frightened, the young mergansers can literally run across the water, raising a plume of spray, wings flapping as they go. The eggs of the harlequin duck have hatched by now, and the young, often found in the same fast water as the mergansers, are about half the size of the adults, and growing rapidly. The young of all the birds, from yellow warbler to golden eagle, rapidly grow feathers, and reach nearly adult size. The yellow warblers take about three weeks, the golden eagles about ten to twelve weeks (Table VIII). In a very short period of time they must learn to fly and must become competent in feeding themselves in preparation for a long migratory flight south. Most young ravens are now self-sufficient, having fledged a month ago. Some crows are still incubating, and some Swainson's hawks are still feeding nestlings. Barn, tree, cliff, and bank swallows have fledged and for a short period of time are fed by their parents before some adults re-nest.

The numbers of young rodents, including Uinta and golden-mantled ground squirrels, red squirrels, and wood and meadow mice, are increasing in numbers and are more frequently seen. The mature male Uinta ground squirrels are now ready to go into

hibernation. The females will
follow about the end of July
when the ground-cover vegetation has definitely turned
brown and the seed heads
of oysterplant are both
conspicuous and numerous.
Young ground squirrels of
the year will disappear into
their prepared burrows by

Uinta Ground Squirrels

mid-August, when much of their forage is gone. No squirrels will
be seen until the following spring. With their disappearance, an
abundant food supply is no longer readily available to raptors.
Prairie falcons feel the pinch and switch to other prey species or
move out of the area. Least chipmunks and jumping mice, both
young and old, are quite active preparing for the coming winter.

The wild rose and stickseed (*Hackelia floribunda*) are in both
flower and fruit. The latter is armed with barbed prickles that
annoyingly stick to clothing, particularly after the burrs have
matured and turned brown. Other plants whose seeds are dispersed in this manner include wild licorice (*Glycyrrhiza lepidota*),
now at peak of flowering, cocklebur (*Xanthium strumarium*),
burdock (*Arctium minus*), and beggarticks *(Bidens cernua)*. More
and more berries, as well as seeds, are developing and maturing.
The berries of the red twinberry honeysuckle and the black twinberry, also a honeysuckle, are ripe. The black berries surrounded
by red bracts look delicious. Although they are not poisonous,

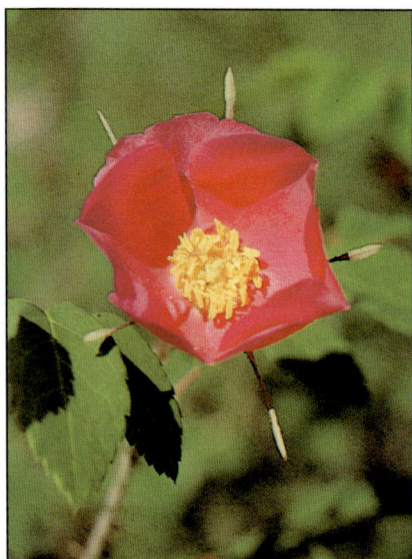

Wild Rose

they are not really edible either. The red ones are edible but insipid. One taste of the now ripening red buffaloberries will be sufficient, even when the berries are bright red and fully ripe. However, various Indian tribes consider these berries a real delicacy, an "Indian ice cream." It's all in the preparation. Try gathering one-quarter cup of berries in late August to early September. To this add a few tablespoons of water and a tablespoon of sugar. Then whip to a froth until it somewhat resembles cotton candy. Having tasted the raw ripe berries, you'll be amazed by the smooth texture and unique taste of this "Indian ice cream." In gathering and preparing the berries, keep them away from grease, oil, and plastic.

At this time when the buffaloberries are turning red, little sunflowers are declining, young western meadowlarks and young tree swallows are fledging, the latter by the hundreds, and the thistles are blooming. The musk thistle blooms first with its array of intimidating thorns and beautiful purple receptacle. This species is soon followed by the dense patches of Canada thistle, a noxious weed that is propagated through seeds that are dispersed by wind and water or by root-runners. Next to appear is

Buffaloberry

the urn-like flower of the bull thistle (*Cirsium vulgare*). These noxious plants, as well as spotted knapweed (*Centaurea maculosa)* and leafy spurge (*Euphorbia esula),* are all introduced weeds, spreading and each year taking over both cultivated and uncultivated lands. They are even invading meadows and native flower gardens of our national parks. Control is a difficult problem. The use of herbicides may temporarily check their spread, but these noxious weeds are no respecters of political or administrative boundaries. Also, the full and adverse affect of herbicides on humans is yet to be tallied. Biological control, the introduction and propagation of insects and parasites that are selective feeders and consume specific weeds such as musk thistle or knapweed, may prove to be effective. An example is the introduction of the musk thistle seed weevil that feeds on the thistle seeds, thus limiting its spread. This balance of nature approach is the most desirable solution on park lands. Further research is underway, and various forms of biological control are being evaluated. But in the long view of things, there is probably little that can be done to eradicate some of these well-established, invading plant species. Some of the more troublesome ones might be detected early and controlled locally. Others will be accepted as naturalized.

The flowers of many exotics are attractive. These include plants such as butter-and-eggs, yellow sweet clover, ox-eye daisy, fever few, leafy spurge, and others already mentioned. Many of these are widespread and are already well established. They line road shoulders and cover fields. They are rapidly spreading and will continue to do so with vigor.

Butter-and-eggs

Golden eagles are fledging, as summer flowers like houndstongue and monkshood are appearing, and as golden aster, woolly yellow daisy, ballhead sandwort, and sego (or mariposa) lily peak. The large dandelion-like seed heads of oysterplant are being eaten by both adult and young pine siskins and goldfinches. The continued flocking of young starlings, cowbirds, Brewer's blackbirds, and tree and cliff swallows are harbingers of approaching fall.

INCREASING NUMBERS of young birds are fledging—white-crowned, vesper, and sage sparrows, yellow-headed blackbirds, yellow-rumped warblers, cliff swallows, western tanagers, house wrens, and mourning doves. Canada geese, having completed molting, are again flying. Some species such as the robin, the American dipper, the mountain bluebird, and the house wren are re-nesting and are feeding a second brood. Young ravens have replaced down with shiny, black feathers. They are now largely independent of their parents who are molting at a time when food in the form of grasshoppers, young birds, and mice is readily available, and domestic chores are over. The molting of wing primaries and tail feathers causes a temporary clumsiness in the raven's flight, but the end result is a shiny, irridescent appearance for the young but full-grown ravens and new flight feathers for the adults. It is a time when adults need an abundance of food for the energy-consuming process of replacing their feathers.

Mink

Young coyotes, red foxes, badgers, minks, pine martens, and weasels learn to catch their prey when the prey are young, inexperienced, and easier to obtain than they will be later. The overall mortality is very high at this time. Animal food is now readily available for both young and adults. So is plant food. Green berries are rapidly developing and some beginning to ripen—those of mountain ash, thimbleberry, baneberry, golden and black currant, chokecherry, serviceberry, holly-grape, elderberry, red-osier dogwwod, berries of twisted-stalk (*Streptopus amplexifolius*), huckleberry (*Vaccinium membranaceum*), whortleberry, wild rosehips, buffaloberry, silverberry, false Solomonseal (*Smilacina racemosum*), and others.

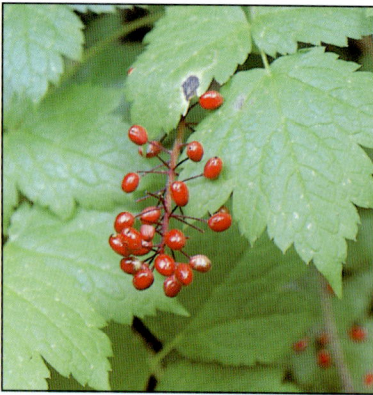

Poisonous Baneberry

The silverberry flowers, silvery on the outside and light yellow within, blend in with the silver leaves. The dry silver-colored fruits are likewise difficult to see even when you are staring at the plant. The berries are largely consumed by wildlife. The shrubs seem to favor stream banks and are common along the Snake River and its tributaries. The bark of these bushes is tough

Monkshood

and fibrous and can readily be pealed off in strips. The strips serve well as cord, or if twisted, as a fishing line or rope. Dogbane can be used in the same way and is found throughout the area, particularly on recently burned-over sites. Try twisting these fiberous strips into a strong length of cord. It will help you to remember or again recognize the plants. The Clark's nutcracker uses the inner bark of juniper (*Juniperus* sp.) to bind together the stick substrata of their nests.

When the monkshood and the columbine are near peak of blooming, some young kestrels are fledging. Early nesting young sharp-shinned hawks have become "branchers," that is they have left the nest and are perched on nearby branches of the nest tree. Juvenile harriers and short-eared owls are still being fed by parents, and the more adventurous ones are moving short distances from the vulnerable nests on the ground. Not only are the young in danger from skunks, badgers, and coyotes at this time, but nests and young are often destroyed when ranchers cut their hay or alfalfa.

Moose calves are now about a month old and staying close to an alert mother. Usually the bulls are separate, but occasionally a family unit of cow, bull, and calf will remain together until disturbed by fall hunters. Elk calves still sport a few spots, although they are now growing fast and depend on speed and alertness rather than on camouflage and lack of motion to avoid danger, such as an attack by a grizzly, a mountain lion, or possibly even a gray wolf in the not too distant future. Very young elk calves minimize their scent dispersal by remaining motionless, sometimes for hours, while their mothers forage at a distance. If by chance you come upon a calf in hiding, do not approach closer, but take a look, possibly snap a picture, and move on.

JANA C. SMITH

Elk Calf

When prince's pine (or wintergreen) is in bloom,
huckleberries are ripe. It is the start of
berry-picking time. As the flowering goldenrod and
yellow sweet clover reach their peak, rabbit-brush
and gumweed are just starting to bloom,
as are the slender hawkweed and silver sagebrush.
By this time most bald eagles have fledged,
but some osprey are still testing their wings
in the nest. In dry summers the landscape is
beginning to change from green to brown.
Grass pollen from timothy flowers is in the air.

FIELDS OF YAMPA are conspicuous with their umbels of small, white flowers born on slender, nearly leafless stems. The plants are now producing and storing starch in their carrot-shaped tubers. The raw tubers are nutlike in taste and a choice food of grizzly bears as well as food-storing rodents. Try them if you can identify them with certainty. They are a bit different, but good. Other plants still in bloom and accumulating food in bulbs, tubers, corms, and roots are wild licorice, sego lily, elk thistle, blue camas, wild hyacinth, wild onions, wild chives (*Allium schoenoprasum*), American bistort (*Polygonum bistortoides*), and others. The fall is the best time of year to utilize these food

Porcupine

sources, as starch is accumulated to produce flowering and leafing the following spring. The bulbs or tubers of such plants as spring beauty, bitterroot (*Lewisia rediviva*), Lewisia, and yellowbell may be located and best used just prior to flowering, before the stored starch is used to produce new spring growth. It is therefore helpful, even necessary, to be able to identify some of these edible plants by early leaves or late summer fruits or pods.

With the mountain hollyhock, bull thistle, and timothy (*Phleum pratense*) at peak of flowering, you can expect to find young Uinta ground squirrels fat and ready for hibernating. Young Swainson's thrushes have fledged, but some young Swainson's hawks have not. Young great gray owls leave the nest before they can fly but continue to be fed by parents. Practically all juvenile kestrels have now fledged. Immature prairie falcons and young red-tailed hawks are still flying and soaring with adults but will soon be foraging entirely on their own. Young ravens are together in small groups and some individuals are being fed by adults, but not necessarily their parents. Others are still perfecting landing techniques. A clumsy landing is a sign of a juvenile bird. The young osprey generally are the latest of the raptors to fledge, and even after leaving their nest they return there to rest and to sleep.

Canada geese have all completed their postnuptial molt and are flying well, some in small premigratory formations. The young of other waterfowl, common mergansers, mallards, American wigeons, Barrow's goldeneyes, and green-winged teals, now have young that are flying and are approaching adult size. Young porcupines are moving out, as evidenced by fresh "blazes" on young trees. Now on their own, the young of many of the small mammals disperse to find food.

It is time to start harvesting berries, beginning with huckleberries or big whortleberries, and terminating with chokecherries, the latter now green. When you find the bitter tasting, red buffaloberries,

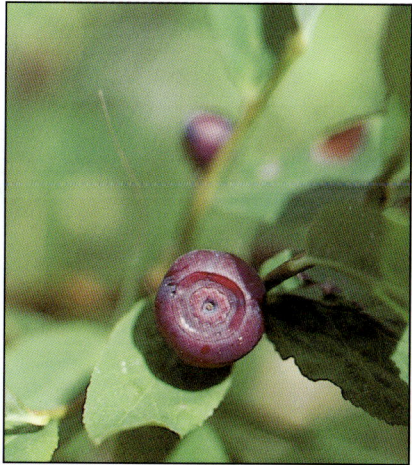

Huckleberry

105

start looking for delicious tasting huckleberries, including the red-berried, low-growing grouse whortleberry—in bloom the first

Tansy

week of June, ready to eat in early August. This is a favorite of bears. They eat the whole plant—berries, stem, and leaves.

Roadside plants, such as butter-and-eggs and mullein (*Verbascum thapsus*), will be in bloom. Bedstraw, alfalfa, spotted knapweed, western coneflower, prickly lettuce (*Lactuca serriola*), and tansy (*Tanacetum vulgare*) are all plants in bloom whose appearance will coincide with some of the events described. For example, when common rabbit-brush (*Chrysothamnus nauseosus*), prince's pine (*Chimaphila umbellata*), and the tansy flower start to bloom, some species of huckleberries, squawbush, and black currants are ripe, and others soon will be. Tansy and rabbit-brush are perennial plants, so if you locate and identify them one year, the next year you can use the flowering of the same individual plants as indicators of the time to pick huckleberries. You might also use the first flowering of pinedrops (*Pterospora andromedea*), a chlorophyll-lacking plant that grows in the same habitat, as an indicator. Also just beginning to bloom are gumweed (*Grindelia squarrosa*), slender hawkweed (*Hieracium gracile*), and silver sagebrush (*Artemisia cana*).

106

The major activity of birds at the nest is over, though some re-nesting occurs among species such as barn, tree, and cliff swallows. Some yellow warblers, white-crowned sparrows, and young osprey are still in the nest, as are some late nesting Swainson's hawks. Young rufous and calliope hummingbirds are abundant, feeding on flowers and at feeders. Fireweed is at peak bloom, and goldeneye and pearly everlasting are common beside hiking trails. Gumweed lines highway shoulders, and western coneflowers are distributed where soils are disturbed.

THERE ARE NOW signs of an altitudinal reversal in time of phenological events. Higher, which until now has meant later, has changed to earlier as fall approaches. Events, instead of progressing upward, are now progressing downward. By mid-August, flowers such as Canada thistle and fireweed peak earlier than those same plants a thousand feet lower. Snowberries at higher elevations are more fully developed than those lower down at the 6,500 foot level. Coloring of a few isolated leaves on trees, shrubs, and herbs herald the coming fall changes, but signs of fall are not yet conspicuous.

Gumweed

As the subtle shift from summer to fall occurs, hummingbirds, young and adults, feed steadily on nectar from the now waning supply of flowers. Many plants have gone to seed, such as bluebonnet, nettle, sticky geranium, stickseed, curlydock (*Rumex crispus*), giant hyssop, (*Agastache urticifolia*), mountain hollyhock, arrowleaf balsamroot, and stonecrop. Flowers still in bloom include fireweed, goldeneye *(Viguiera multiflora)*,

108

pearly everlasting *(Anaphalis margaritacea)*, and western coneflowers *(Rudbeckia occidentalis)*.

Raspberries and a number of currants are now ripe. Elderberries, rose hips, juniper berries, and silverberries are ripening. The bright orange berries of fairybells and the orange-red berries of twisted-stalk are now ripe, as blue-flow-ered lettuce (*Lactuca pulchella*) appears. Rushpink (*Lygodesmia*

Coneflower

grandiflora) colors rocky stream banks where it is encountered by anglers. Prince's pine reaches a peak in its shaded, timbered

Twisted Stalk Berry

environment as does silver sagebrush in the more open sagebrush-grass habitat.

When the rabbit-brush is approaching its peak of blooming, coloring the landscape with bright yellow composite flowers, and when a few splotches of fall colors show up in trees and understory vegetation, bull elk are still shedding the velvet from their antlers, and an occasional early bugle call can be heard in the distance. Some osprey have now fledged, cliff swallows have left, grasshoppers are quite numerous, and cutthroat trout are taking both real and artificial flies. Fly fishing in the Snake River drainage is excellent and will continue to be good as river hawthorn berries ripen, turning red, later black, a nibble for the angler.

FLOCKS OF IMMATURE starlings and blackbirds are increasing in size while the drab-colored starlings are molting to their dark adult plumage. Immature mountain bluebirds, as well as many species of swallows, are congregating and flocking. Most great blue herons have fledged and the later-hatching young of common mergansers are full grown and beginning to fly in family groups. Sage grouse young are nearly full grown and are attracted to water as their environment dries up. Stoneflies continue to emerge from the nymphal stage about the time the yellow flowers of gumweed and beggarticks are commonly seen. Uinta ground squirrels have disappeared, now hibernating in their burrows. In contrast, least chipmunks, golden-mantled ground squirrels, and deer mice are increasingly active and more visible as they store large caches of a variety of seeds for winter consumption.

Some late-flowering plants such as hawkweed, Engelmann aster (*Aster engelmannii*), arrowleaf groundsel *(Senecio triangularis)*, butterweed groundsel *(Senecio serra)*, water groundsel *(Senecio hydrophilus)*, goldenrods, water speedwell (*Veronica anagallis-aquatica*), and Hornemann willowweed (*Epilobium hornemannii*) are still coming into bloom.

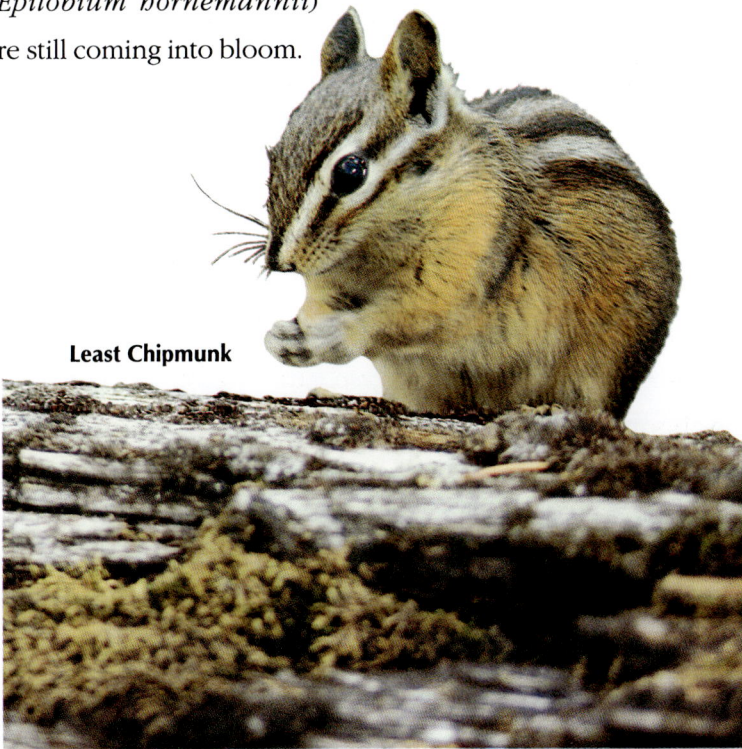

Least Chipmunk

MICHAEL S. SAMPLE

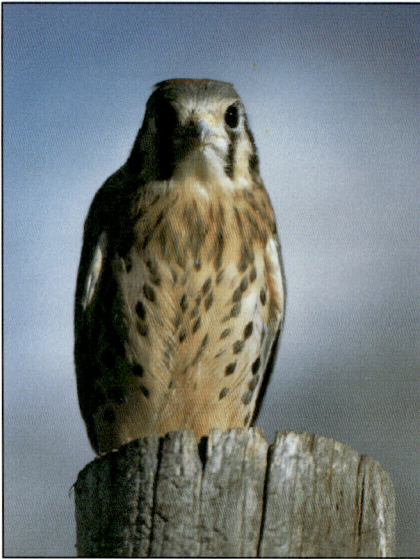

Young American Kestrel

Others which appeared earlier, harebell, yarrow, shrubby cinquefoil, musk thistle, and henbane (*Hyoscyamus niger*), still persist. Elk thistles and seed heads of mules-ears are now brown and dead. Yellow leaves of wyethia and the red ones of geranium give color to the understory foliage.

Prince's pine is in fruit, and serviceberries are now ripe and dark blue, mealy, and, in seasons of adequate moisture, tasty. If huckleberries are scarce, as periodically happens, mix those you have picked with serviceberries, and you will still get a stronger and tastier flavor of huckleberry in your jelly. You will probably want to remove the few, but larger, serviceberry seeds during the jelly-making process.

Thimbleberries and wild red raspberries are still ripening. Young Swainson's hawks have fledged. They may often be seen perching on fence posts waiting for their parents to feed them. They, like the great gray owls, are quite tame, allowing human observers to approach quite closely. Kestrels are teaching their young to hunt, and crows are flying in small flocks. With a startling whirr of wings, sage grouse are rising out of the sagebrush in growing numbers, apparently a result of families getting together. They regularly congregate where water is available.

The activities of pronghorn, elk, mule deer, and moose are centered around caring for their young.

Elk Cow and Calf

Almost all berries are now ripe, including red-osier dogwood, silverberry, and mountain ash, all three for the birds rather than for human consumption. Golden currants, serviceberries, and the blue holly-grapes are ready for picking at the time mountain hollyhock and blue flax are about finished blooming. Fringed sagebrush and some big sagebrush are just coming into flower when buck pronghorn are chasing young males away from their growing harems.

THE YOUNG OF MOST bird species raised in the area are still present but are secretive, less vocal, and more difficult to see and identify than when their activities are centered around a nest. A few species, such as late or re-nesting barn swallows and robins, are still incubating eggs or brooding young. Pikas are busy cutting and curing a variety of grasses and herbs, arranging them in "haystacks" to dry before storing them underground for winter use. Red squirrels (or chickarees) are consuming seeds from the green, unopened lodgepole pine cones and are caching huge piles of other cones as well as seeds. Black bears and grizzly bears will raid these middens, thus acquiring fat for later use during hibernation. Least chipmunks are filling their cheek pouches with seeds of grasses, shrubs, and herbs as they busily transport them to winter caches. White-footed deer mice are doing the same in preparation for winter and are still raising litters of young.

Pika

In Jackson Hole, the now separate bands of pronghorns, led by a dominant buck, will, after breeding, gradually assemble into larger groups before migrating out of the area. This preparation for movement to winter range is occasionally delayed. Deep snow then takes its toll of the herd—both of those animals that remain and those that try to leave.

Antelope

The total number of bird and mammal life in the area is at a peak from which it will now decline due to death and migration. Predation is a major decimating force on this late-summer-fall population. Predators such as badgers and martens are now breeding, continuing a biological process that will result in a new generation of predators by spring (Table VII). Badgers, as well as martens, breed in late summer and autumn, but implantation of the fertilized egg is delayed until mid-winter. The young are born in March and early April, a far more favorable time for birth than would be the case were there no delay in embryo development following conception (Table VII).

At this time of year a hard early frost can accelerate, but diminish, the process of fall coloring. It can start the dropping of frosted, but still-green leaves, thus creating an early but colorless autumn season.

An early fall with a dearth of color is a result of inclement weather, but the fall season itself with its noticeable and sequential changes is due to climatic influences, such as shorter days, diminishing light, and lower temperatures—these caused by the inclination of the earth while revolving around the sun. Bright, long-lasting fall colors are a result of warm, sunny days and cool nights. These alter movement of water within the plants, resulting in an increase of carbohydrates in the leaves. Green chlorophyll breaks down and pigments such as carotene, anthocyanin (red), and xanthophyll (yellow) become visible.

*Sagebrush pollens are in the air causing hay fever
and asthma symptoms in some people, this at a
time when cones of the five-needled pines are
opening. The attractive but noxious exotic weeds,
knapweed and tansy, are at their peak of
flowering. Bull elk are sparring and testing their
antlers as the mating season continues and the
hunting season approaches. Grasshoppers and other
insects are still numerous and cutthroat trout are
feeding on the surface. Blackbirds, starlings,
and western meadowlarks are flocking. Most
chokecherry leaves have turned yellow, making it
easy to locate the bushes and the cherries, which
are now red. The mourning cloak, one of the early
appearing butterflies, is still encountered. Some of
these will hibernate. They tend to congregate on
aspen trees where wood borers have caused
the sap to ooze.*

BY THE TIME most American white pelicans have fledged,
sandhill crane families have left their nesting area and young
mergansers are flocking. The young of osprey are fledging, hummingbirds are decreasing in numbers, and beavers have young

Beaver

about the size of muskrats, still small enough to ride on one parent's back as the parents swim up through fast water. The emphasis is now switching from care and protection of the young beavers to preparing for winter. They are now building major dams and enlarging pond lodges, raising water levels, and creating channels that radiate out from the lodge to nearby preferred sources of food: willow, aspen, cottonwood, and alder.

The marsh sow thistle (*Sonchus arvensis)* is simultaneously in bloom and in fruit. Where you find these silky, white seed heads, you may notice that dry ground areas you traversed in spring are now flooded. Working methodically and at first unobtrusively, the beaver has altered this habitat to fit his needs. Next spring you may locate common snipe and various ducks nesting in a territory previously used by yellow warblers and Brewer's blackbirds.

The resinous cones of the five-needled pines, the whitebark

Chokecherry

(*Pinus albicaulis*), and the limber pine *(Pinus flexilis)*, are now opening, attracting Clark's nutcrackers, Steller's jays, blue grouse, red squirrels, chipmunks, and other wildlife forms. All are busy gathering, consuming, and storing the maturing seeds that are rich in fat and protein. Some seeds are pried out of the cones by Clark's nutcrackers, while others are picked up by blue grouse feeding on the ground. Black and grizzly bears are attracted to this rich source of food. Bears often get first servings by breaking off green cones and eating them whole, including the sticky resin. Nut crops vary; some years there is a tremendous supply, other years practically none. Pine nuts are thus a rich and a bounteous food source but not always a dependable one. This is also the case with buffaloberries, huckleberries, and chokecherries. In

119

years when nut and berry crops fail, the grizzlies wander further in their foraging, are lean and hungry, and thus, often more aggressive. A hungry bear is a dangerous bear. The status of the nut or berry crop should be considered and could possibly affect your backpacking plans.

Within the Greater Yellowstone Ecosystem, the whitebark pines with their purple cones grow in the spruce-fir formation or sub-alpine zone, the whitebark at a slightly higher altitude than the limber. The limber pine seeds drop earlier, and the cones remain on the trees. Here, the two-needled, shade-intolerant lodgepole pine is a passing stage toward the climax vegetation. The five-needled pines develop toward a climax or exist as a long persisting sub-climax stage, growing up under and in the shade of lodgepole pines. Heat from fire opens the lodgepole cones, and the seeds are immediately and widely disseminated by the wind. This is not so with the heavy nut-seeds of the five-needled pine. The seeds or "pine nuts" come from unburned islands of timber or from mature trees on the periphery of a burn. The seeds are slowly dispersed and some buried, others scattered by the foraging and caching activities of birds, particularly Clark's nutcrackers. The 1988 Yellowstone fires eliminated thousands of these trees at an age when they were just beginning to form a young whitebark pine forest. It will take years before new trees bear abundant nuts, but the potential for the growth of a new, five-needled pine forest exists. The Clark's nutcrackers will hasten this process.

Whitebark Pine (tallest tree in foreground)

When the berries of mountain ash have attained a bright orange color, sandhill cranes are flocking and calling, preparing to migrate out of the nesting area. A rare whooping crane may be moving south, stopping a few days enroute.
The fall hawk migration is beginning with a few kestrels, Cooper's, marsh, and sharp-shinned hawks moving leisurely through, stopping temporarily where there is an abundant food supply. Young yellow-rumped and yellow warblers, pine siskins, young northern flickers, a variety of young sparrows, bluebirds, swallows, rodents, grasshoppers, and other insects are all available for food at this time.

THE MATURING of white, spongy snowberries can be used as an indicator that fall bird migration, at first slowly, then dramatically, is altering the bird population of Jackson Hole and surrounding areas. As this avian migration begins with a trickle of birds moving south, the large mammal rutting season manifests itself sporadically in the behavior of various species. Should you now answer the grunt-like call of a bull moose you may start him moving toward you and wind up face to face with an angry moose, still some velvet on his huge antlers, the hair on his back raised, ears back. He may give you little choice but to climb a tree, particularly if you continue to imitate his grunts. At this time when

you may hear the bugling of the bull elk, the bleat of the cows, and the grunts of bull moose, you may also, day or night, listen entranced to the chorus of one or more families of coyotes. Their yips and howls magnify their actual numbers—perhaps in this way throwing fear into their potential prey.

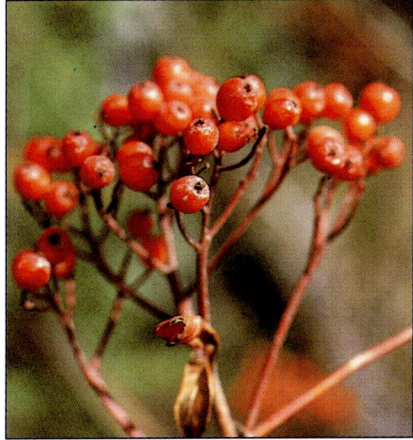

Mountain Ash Berries

Mature bull elk are now challenging one another as they build up, or take over, harems, depending on the outcome of a battle. The very high-pitched bugle of spike or young bull elk may be heard as they futilely and half-heartedly challenge the dominant bulls. Mule deer, like the elk, are rubbing their new antlers against small saplings and bushes to remove the velvet. Buck pronghorns are becoming ever more vigilant in acquiring and maintaining a harem. Even as these rutting season activities become more and more pronounced, a second brood of barn swallows may be about to leave the nest. Will their still abundant insect food supply hold out until they are ready to migrate? Juvenile Swainson's hawks are flying well, but are still calling for food from the parents. Immature red-tailed hawks are now on their own, living off

Bull Moose

grasshoppers and Mormon crickets when unable to catch enough young field or white-footed mice. Adult and young ground squirrels have disappeared. Resident birds raised in the area now have to compete for food with the migrants that are passing through.

Many flowers now blooming are scattered, single remnants growing in favored sites—plants such as harebell, Indian paintbrush, yellow monkeyflower (*Mimulus guttatus*), beggarticks, coneflower, geranium, giant hyssop, scarlet gilia, yarrow, lupine, tansy, thistles, and a variety of asters and daisies. The flower gardens are gone, in some cases replaced by fields of silvery-white seed-tufts of fireweed. Many plants now have dry brown brittle leaves and stems. In a dry fall this is a bane to hunters as it is difficult to stalk game without making noise and alerting the quarry. When the Wyoming elk hunting season opens it often coincides with a definite coloring of deciduous trees and the understory bushes, shrubs, and herbs.

Some grizzlies, perhaps influenced by a drop in temperature, may start early to dig a winter den at the base of a large tree, usually a conifer located on a north facing slope. With subsequent changes in weather, they may move back to more profitable foraging areas such as grass-sagebrush habitats where they prey on meadow voles and dig up bulbs of melica grass *(Melica bulbosa)*. Here in open country they can be spotted and readily observed. For another two months the grizzlies continue to put on layers of fat, their food supply for the long winter, which for them lasts five to six months. Winter will last nine months for the Uinta ground squirrels.

Mount Moran

Autumn leaves are turning color, changing rapidly as influenced by drought, moisture, and frost. When you see the yellow aspen leaves, the elk bugling should be at its peak and most audible on cold clear nights. The bulls are vigorously guarding their harems and large pronghorn males are doing the same, mating with various females as opportunity offers. An early snow skiff may whiten the ground, making tracking possible and hunting easier. Outside of protected areas, big game species have become wary, hard to observe and approach. Summer resident birds are somewhat numerous, and migrants are moving through. These are birds that must complete their annual cycle in a warmer clime.

WITH THE ARRIVAL of the fall equinox, the decreasing amount of daylight produces hormonal changes in the bull elk that result in the swelling of their necks, bugling, and behavioral changes—such as aggression, urine spraying, antler rubbing, and rounding up of harems. All of this behavior is a part of the rut.

As fall days become shorter and cooler, manufacturing of chlorophyll by plants is retarded. Thus, when chlorophyll

Bugling Elk

MICHAEL S. SAMPLE

Aspen Leaf

destruction exceeds production, yellow pigments show up in the leaves, having been previously concealed by the green chlorophyll. In many species, such as Rocky Mountain maple, some huckleberries, and river hawthorn, anthocyanin pigments develop with the onset of cool weather, producing the red and purple colors. The landscape through individual shrubs, herbs, and trees takes on a mosaic of spectacular color. Most aspen leaves are yellow, but some orange; serviceberry are yellow and red; hawthorn are red and orange; rose are yellow and red; snowberry leaves are yellow; geranium are red with some yellow; huckleberry are red and yellow; cherry are yellow and red; baneberry leaves are yellow; and fireweed are red, yellow, and orange. Yellow leaves are showing up among the still-green willows and narrowleaf cottonwoods. The understory of higher bushes and young trees is predominantly in colors of yellow, orange, and red. Leaves of the aspen and cottonwoods do not produce anthocyanins and therefore turn only yellow, though tannins in the yellow leaves may produce a golden-brown or orange effect. Tannins in red leaves result in a purplish color, as in red-osier. Eventually, with decomposition of the pigments, only tannins remain in the leaves, giving the landscape a distinctly brown aspect. Frost hastens the arrival of this final stage followed by defoliation, but cool weather, not frost, is conducive to full development of fall coloring. Alders turn yellow but usually later than do most trees. Quite often they turn brown without coloring.

Silverberries are mature, as are also the white, spongy snowberries and the red-mottled berries of false Solomonseal. The black berries of twinberry honeysuckle are now shrivelled, and a few dried serviceberries and currants still adhere to the parent shrubs. Many rose hips are ripe for picking, but chokecherries are not.

As the landscape takes on color, blackbirds, cowbirds, and meadowlarks may be seen flocking. Young crows and ravens of the year fly in small but continually growing flocks. Canada geese are more frequently flying in "V" formations. Sage sparrows, yellow and yellow-rumped warblers, and mountain bluebirds are feeding and flying in small flocks. Numerous species of passerine birds are present, their numbers attracting an occasional migrating merlin or peregrine falcon, as well as the more numerous sharp-shinned and Cooper's hawks. Some of these immature raptors, like merlins, migrate through the ecosystem within a few days of the same time each year. Local nesting osprey are still fishing the north and south forks of the Snake River and sections of the Yellowstone River near their nest sites.

Bald eagles, both mature and immature, patrol the Snake and other rivers hunting or scavenging for food. They tend to limit their foraging to aquatic habitats and in some areas make daily

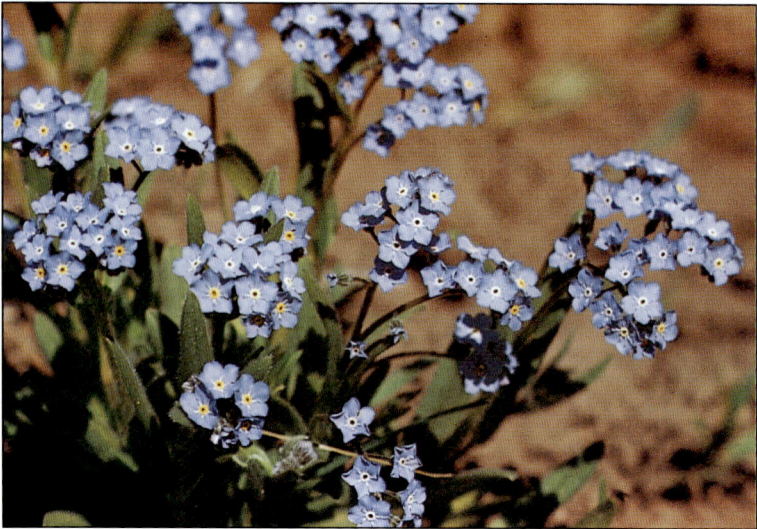

Forget-me-nots

visits to ponds, lake shores, and marsh lands, which harbor a variety of waterfowl, some of which have been wounded during the hunting season. Under these conditions, the eagles are often successful in getting a meal. On one occasion, I watched them stoop on rafts of ducks and coots, then circle low and come in for another pass. Just as it appeared that the eagle had a coot in its outstretched talons, the coots would dive as one bird and remain submerged until the eagle had flown by. Time and time again the persistent eagle would circle, attack, miss its prey and try again. The eagle appeared to be attempting to snag a coot just as it popped up or took off. The eagle definitely avoided getting wet. Lots of calories were burned without the effort being successful. The bald eagle appears to make out better by feeding on carrion than it does by taking live prey.

Though night temperatures may have dropped well below

freezing, frogs and garter snakes can still be encountered. They are a component of the eagle's warm weather diet. Affected by the cold and thus slow to move, they are vulnerable to predators unless they find a secure hideout to await the warmer mid-day temperatures.

An assortment of plants is still in bloom; the flowers widely scattered. Some of these include:

big sagebrush	mountain hollyhock
bittercress	mullein
bluebonnet lupine	musk thistle
bull thistle	ox-eye daisy
Canada thistle	pearly everlasting
common rabbit-brush	pleated gentian
common tansy	primrose
douglas rabbitbrush	rushpink
Engelmann aster	shore buttercup
false dandelion	shrubby cinquefoil
fever few	spotted knapweed
forget-me-not	sticky geranium
giant hyssop	thickstem aster
goldeneye	water buttercup
goldenrod	water groundsel
goldenweed	water ladysthumb
gumweed	water speedwell
harebell	western aster
hoary aster	western fringed gentian
hop-trefoil	yarrow
lodgepole lupine	yellow evening primrose
matchbrush	yellow monkeyflower
mountain bluebell	yellow sweet clover
mountain dandelion	

Fall colors are approaching or are at their peak when you see flocks of robins avidly feeding on chokecherries or the berries of the river hawthorn. Bull elk are regularly bugling and cows calling as large bulls amass a harem. Warblers, finches, immature bluebirds, doves, sapsuckers, starlings, cowbirds, and flickers are numerous, as are the southward migrating hawks preying on them. It is the time of the autumnal equinox when day and night are again of equal length, a time when a hard frost can shorten the period of fall colors or clement weather extend it. Light snowfalls are not only possible but likely and tend to stimulate flocking and bird migrations.

THE REVERSAL OF flowering events is underway, with some plants at higher altitudes finishing blooming earlier than the same species at a lower altitude. This first becomes evident at about the time fireweed reaches a peak of blooming (August 7-13). It becomes even more noticeable with the autumn coloring of leaves at the beginning of the fall equinox with its decreasing daylight—those plants at higher altitudes and latitudes generally coloring before the same species lower down. This is due in part to lowering

Red-winged Blackbirds

temperatures, which in mountainous regions decrease an average of about 3 degrees for each 1,000 foot increase in elevation.

The first fall colors appear at the higher latitudes and altitudes and take the form of a patchwork quilt moving southward and downward over the countryside. When the colors fade or are gone in Alaska and northern Canada, they are approaching the peak of coloring in the Jackson Hole area of Wyoming and south into the Southern Rockies.

Female cowbirds, starlings, and other blackbirds are forming in ever larger flocks. Many resident hawks have left summer territories, and others such as Cooper's and sharp-shinned hawks and northern harriers are migrating south. Local Swainson's hawks have departed, and young great horned owls are hunting and on their own, but still filling the night air with their baby hunger calls, no longer diligently heeded by the parents. Most prairie falcons have left the area by about mid-August when their main food, Uinta ground squirrels, went underground. Hummingbirds have disappeared as flowers are now few and far between, many in seed or represented by dry brown stems and leaves.

The rounded stickseeds of houndstongue now cling tenaciously to socks, trousers, and even shoes, as do the burrs of stickseed or false forget-me-not. Western coneflower is in seed, so is bull thistle, geranium, lupine, tansy, henbane, little sunflower, mountain hollyhock, green gentian, elk thistle, and fireweed, to mention only a few. Some plants still in bloom are harebell, goldenrods, goldeneye, giant hyssop, mountain dandelion, and rabbit-brush.

Grasshoppers become active as the day temperatures rise. Dry-fly and nymph fishing for cutthroat trout and whitefish is excellent in the Snake, Gros Ventre, and other rivers of the ecosystem. Osprey may still be seen near nest sites or observed fishing the Snake River. Least chipmunks are eating and storing snowberries and the seeds of bitterbrush. Rose hips are ripe and ready for picking. The vitamin C-rich berries make delicious jelly. They are consumed by many forms of wildlife, and some are available well into winter, even after they are blanketed with snow.

*When fall colors are fading, flowers disappearing,
and mountain ash, big whortleberry, and geranium
leaves are red, it is time to prepare for the fall
brown trout fishing. These trout are moving out of
the lakes to spawning sites, the males matching the
peak of fall coloring with their brilliant spawning
hues. It is a period of sunny days, chilly nights,
panoramas of fading color, migrating birds, big
game animals in the rut, and wildlife and man
preparing for winter; too much to see and do, hard
choices to make—hiking, birding, fishing, hunting,
boating, or getting in winter firewood. (The latter
a task, but also a recreational activity.)*

CONTINUING AND STILL dominating the scene at perhaps
the most enjoyable time of year is the attractive but fading foliage.
For example, the brown flower stalks of green gentian are even
more conspicous in seed than in bloom. With this is the continued flocking of birds ready to migrate and interesting sightings of
those passing through—yellow-rumped warblers, dark-eyed juncos, pine siskins, American goldfinches, mountain bluebirds,
red-winged blackbirds, common nighthawks, European starlings
in dark adult plumage, and a constant trickle of hawks. A few

osprey and kestrels are still present, the latter feeding on grass-hoppers and Mormon crickets. Migrating harriers, Cooper's and red-tailed hawks, find ample prey at a bounteous time of year. White-crowned sparrows as well as green-tailed towhees have departed their summer haunts. Red-naped sapsuckers are gird-ling young aspens before the sap stops flowing. Mourning cloak butterflies seek out the even-spaced ring of holes, attracted by the oozing sap. Girdling by sapsuckers, though apparently beneficial to some insects, such as the mourning cloak butterfly, is often detrimental in other ways. Girdling kills limbs and even entire trees. The horticulturist, though an ornithologist, may not in this instance be a bird enthusiast.

Lake trout (Mackinaw) and brown trout, both introduced by man to the region, are beginning their movements into spawning areas, the browns from lakes into gravel bars in the streams, the lake trout to rocky bottoms along lake shores. Both species can be readily taken by drifting streamer flies, deep and close to the bottom. This spawning movement will grow and increase as days shorten and water temperatures drop. Brook trout, a species introduced from the East, spawn at about the same time. All must try to protect their eggs from the Rocky Mountain whitefish, a native of the trout family that also spawns in the fall.

Flowers are now scarce, but as you float the trout waters or hike the river shorelines, you will see a few hardy, late-blooming individuals such as rushpink, pleated and western fringed gentian, water buttercup, shore buttercup, water speedwell, water groundsel, marsh sow thistle, and the water-loving forget-me-not, with its bright blue, yellow-centered flowers. These are flowers of the autumn angler.

Bull elk are still guarding their harems, and bull and cow moose can be observed mating and may still be seen in a

Brown Trout

MICHAEL S. SAMPLE

family group if not separated and disturbed by hunters. On one occasion I watched a vigilant cow moose act as sentinel and protector to her spent mate who was resting nearby in the willows. Approaching too close under these conditions, I triggered an attack by the cow. Her tactics were to charge, ears back, then rising up on her hind feet attempt to come down on me with her large, lethal front hoofs—a weapon well-worth avoiding. Pronghorns continue to mate with members of their tightly controlled harems.

Young grizzly bears, males under five years of age in particular, tend to wander, in order to find now scarce nuts, berries, green forage, and rodents. Pine nuts are now gone, but bulbs such as those of onion grass, and small rodents, are available, usually in open country. The need to accumulate fat for winter hibernation is the driving force that keeps the bears moving and foraging day and night. In lean years, they may become unusually aggressive. A hungry grizzly is a potentially dangerous bear, a fact to keep in mind in grizzly country.

Grizzly Bears

Some tansy plants and a few thickstem asters, along with Indian paintbrush, yarrow, forget-me-not, arnica, and the persistent dandelion, occasionally brighten the brown ground cover with blotches of color. Nights are noticeably cooler at eighteen to twenty degrees. Lengthening nights and skim ice induce the beaver to start to cut, haul, and stash a winter supply of willow shoots.

Ducks and geese are moving south. Brown and brook trout are spawning in increasing numbers. Elk, moose, mule deer, and pronghorn are mating as narrowleaf cottonwoods continue dropping their leaves and fall colors generally fade. Bighorn sheep are grazing alpine meadows located close to cliff retreats, the rams and ewes still in separate bands.

SOME BIRDS ARE STILL congregating in flocks, while others such as the yellow-rumped warbler are passing through in migration. Most greater sandhill cranes have gone south on their way to New Mexico via Grays Lake National Refuge in Idaho. Mountain bluebirds, both mature and immature, are conspicuously flitting from one fencepost to another. Red crossbills can be heard and seen periodically. An occasional dandelion, yarrow, or thickstem aster bloom gives a spark of color to the largely brown and brittle ground-cover vegetation. In wet habitat, water groundsel does the same.

With the fading of fall colors there is a noticeable tapering off in the elk rut, evidenced by the rapid drop-off in bugling. No longer can the hunter, photographer, or wildlife enthusiast readily get an answering challenge to his imitation call. Apparently, one

Bighorn Rams

Grizzly Bear, Coyote, and Elk Carcass

function of this bugling is to intimidate rival bulls and attract mates. A large dominant bull may attract and busily herd a harem of over thirty cows. Such a bull, moving close in response to call and counter-call, will spar, then lock antlers in an effort to push or force his antagonist to his knees. Most such duels end in one combatant conceding defeat with little or no real injury. However, in some cases, a sharp-pointed, bony tine is forcefully driven into the neck or body, resulting in serious injury or death. The once vigorous elk will provide high protein meals for hungry grizzlies or black bears about to hibernate. It is possible that the winner may also be a loser as he must continue to defend his harem while still guarding and breeding his cows. He loses weight, becomes gaunt and spent by the time the rut is over. If he fails to regain his strength and vigor he may succumb to the rigors of winter.

141

Elk calling is not allowed in national parks except under special hunting permit arrangements. It is allowed on national forest lands. Whether you are a hunter or a wildlife observer, bugling a bull elk from a distance, luring him on with repeated calls complete with stamping, grunting, and breaking of branches, is a real thrill. It is possible to entice an aroused bull to respond as though you were pulling him in on a string. There are the repeated calls followed by periods of silence, and then suddenly and quietly the antlered giant appears out of the dark timber and moves to less than a stone's throw from you, the white-polished antler tips reflecting the rising sun. Do you just watch in awe? Do you snap a photograph or do you raise a rifle? In a flash he is gone. Was he real or an apparition? The snapping of branches answers the query.

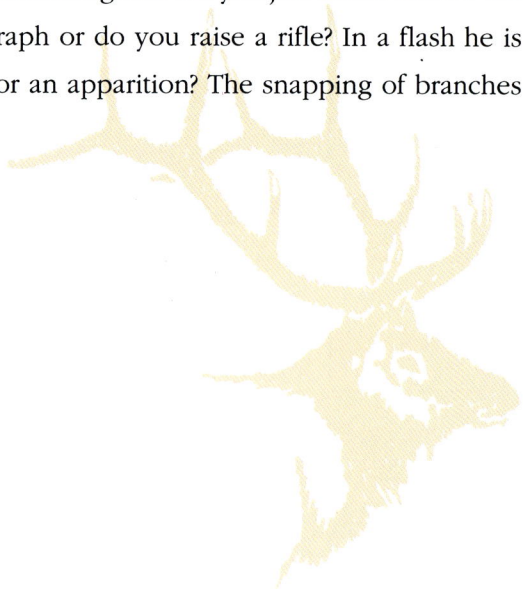

All the ungulates or big game species are now
in some stage (mule deer early, pronghorn late)
of their rut. Fall colors are gone or fading;
most leaves have fallen. Plant life begins
to enter a dormant period.

MULE DEER BUCKS are starting into the rutting season, bull elk are well along but still bugling, and pronghorn bucks are herding their harems but with less vigilance. Some high-flying geese formations are going south. Brown trout are still moving to spawning areas in increasing numbers, and most males are now highly colored, the time of coloring and spawning activity influenced by water temperatures.

Mountain bluebirds and a few yellow-rumped warblers are still present, the bluebirds seemingly reluctant to leave as long as insects are available. Cabbage butterflies and Mormon crickets are still active. The crickets seek the sun's warmth emanating from the black macadam roads. The heat makes them active, but the open roads leave them vulnerable to young ravens and magpies who prey on them as other food sources dwindle.

Starlings in flocks of two to three hundred birds rise from the fields and bank and wheel in unison as they perfect their formation flying. Trees, bare of leaves, are suddenly replenished with dark

JANA C. SMITH

Canada Geese

fluttering foliage as the circling starlings swoop in and alight. Born in the Yellowstone area, starlings seem an integral part of the natural environment, yet forty years ago none nested or wintered here. They compete with native species and in urban areas foul the trees and buildings where they roost in large numbers. This is an example of the rapid adaptation of a smart, aggressive, exotic species to a foreign, yet favorable, environment. In vast numbers the starlings are no more welcome than is the Canada thistle. Change, however, is inevitable, but informed management anticipates such changes and the consequences.

Least chipmunks are storing winter food as a few migrating red-tailed hawks and northern harriers hunt their way south, occasionally taking an unwary chipmunk, who in his foraging for more seeds has exposed himself to danger and to sudden death.

Mule Deer Buck

*Occasional storms temporarily blanket the area
with snow, causing grizzly bears to move to den
sites or to previously prepared hibernation dens.
Some black bears will already have hibernated.
Ice forming on ponds and streams alters
concentration of waterfowl, moving them
to faster water. Migrant ducks and geese fly
in from the north, their stay temporary
before they wing their way farther south.*

IMMATURE COMMON mergansers continue to gather in flocks
before migrating. Some adults remain where there is open water
throughout the winter. This is also the habitat of the American
dipper. Trumpeter swans increase in number on Flat Creek in the
National Elk Refuge, Yellowstone National Park, and at the Red
Rock Lakes area. Migrating tundra swans can arrive any day now
on their way south. Geese and white pelicans are passing through,
flying high in formation. A solitary dandelion, wild strawberry, or
long-leafed phlox bloom may yet be seen. Neither pronghorn
antelope nor sage grouse have yet left Jackson Hole for winter
range in windswept sagebrush habitats, but some grouse in flocks
will do so soon.

Cattle, that in spring were trailed to grazing allotments on

White-footed Mouse

Forest Service land, are now moving down prior to round-up and shipment from ranches to stockyards. Coyotes, drifting down with the cattle, feed on the mice disturbed by the grazing activities. These include the white-footed mouse and both the meadow and long-tailed voles. If fortunate, you may hear the coyotes barking and yapping in the distance.

Snow moves down the mountain slopes, briefly covering the valleys with a white blanket before receding upward to higher elevations. In yo-yo fashion it will move down and up with passing storms, but will relentlessly creep down until it remains on the valley floors. Winter arrives and stays.

Black Bear

Beavers are still busily adding to their winter
cache of food before ice puts an end to this activity.
Mountain bluebirds have departed, starlings are
still flocking, a few red-tailed hawks are moving
through the ecosystem, most osprey have flown
south, and some northern shrikes are appearing as
a population of winter resident birds develops.
Big game, upland bird, and waterfowl hunting
activities predominate. Mountain whitefish are
schooling up in deep riffles and pools. The females
are fat with eggs and ready to spawn, as brown
trout spawning reaches a peak.

BOTH WATER AND AIR temperatures are such that ice may
form on your fishing rod guides with nearly every cast. To free
your line, it may be necessary to dunk your rod in the relatively
warmer water.

Mountain whitefish are so closely packed in some pools that
anglers using weighted triple hooks or metal lures could snag one
at almost every cast. Large populations of whitefish were thought
to compete with the native cutthroat trout and thus considered
detrimental to maintaining optimum trout populations. Hence,
fall snagging of the widely distributed whitefish was, until

recently, encouraged in some streams. However, at this time of year whitefish can be readily taken on small dry flies, a variety of small nymphs, or even on large streamer flies used for brown trout. The best success is with small hooks, as the whitefish, because of its tiny snout-like mouth, has difficulty taking in larger ones. The whitefish is underrated both as a sport and pan fish. A two-pound fish puts up a credible fight and, when feeding voraciously on a hatch of small midges, can be exasperatingly difficult to hook. Persistent rumor has it that whitefish are bony and not good to

Whitefish

eat. Some anglers confuse them with the squaw fish, a bony member of the minnow family. The bone structure of the white-fish is similar to that of trout, and the cooked meat is white and delicious. Therefore, they should be managed as a desirable, native sport fish.

The key to enjoying a meal of whitefish is in the preparation. They should be skinned, an easier task than scaling. They can be filleted, but are equally delicious broiled or roasted whole. Try them covered with a batter of crumbs and mayonnaise or sour cream. If you have listened to derogatory propaganda, you'll be pleasantly surprised. They are excellent cooked fresh or smoked.

Bald eagles from the northern latitudes migrate into the Jackson Hole area and other parts of the Greater Yellowstone Ecosystem, attracted by spawning fish and elk gut piles in areas open to hunting. The first rough-legged hawks from the north appear and hunt meadow voles as long as snow depths permit. A few dandelions will be visible until permanently covered by snow. This hardy and prolific plant may be the first flower you see in spring and the last in fall.

WINTERING BALD EAGLE numbers build up in the state of Wyoming to between 600 and 800 birds, as both mature and immature eagles move into the ecosystem from as far away as Canada. These eagles mingle with resident nesters, concentrating around elk kills. Just how these migrants know where food is available, and when, is a mystery. Like bears, they seem to have a remarkable ability for recalling such information and acting on it. When a food source dwindles, the eagles disperse but will return when food again becomes abundant. The Jackson Hole fall and winter concentrations of bald eagles, though small (twenty birds), are comparable to larger ones along the Skagit River in Washington, the Missouri River near Helena, Montana, and the

MICHAEL S. SAMPLE

Bald Eagle

3,000 or more eagles congregated along a few miles of the Chilkat River in Alaska.

Trout fishing in the Snake River is over until April, but the season for whitefish is year round. Brook trout, brown trout, and whitefish are still spawning. Lake trout season re-opens November 1 with completion of lake trout spawning. Fishing from lake shores is excellent, but chilly.

Young great gray owls have dispersed and are hunting singly. The long-tailed weasel is changing into an ermine—half white, half brown.

Great Gray Owl

151

When the rough-legged hawks from the north put in an appearance, look for elk moving down from higher summer and fall ranges. Winter storms seem to bring in these hawks that have nested in the far north. The storms often coincide with the final movement of the widely dispersed bands of elk approaching their winter range, the National Elk Refuge. With snow on the ground and temperatures below freezing, the grizzlies will go into hibernation.

THE FINAL STAGES of the southern elk herd migration may transpire within a few days or stretch out for a week or more, depending on timing and severity of current and previous snow storms. The final migratory movements of the elk are often at night, leaving only a trail of hoof prints or scattered snow across a highway to inform the early morning hunter that the elk have passed. Broken buck and wire fences tell not only the hunter, but also the disgruntled rancher, that the elk are moving. Good news for one is bad news for the other!

When you observe a flying or soaring buteo that looks different from the red-tailed and Swainson's hawks you have observed throughout the summer, you may suspect that it is a rough-legged

Migrating Elk

hawk (formerly American rough-legged hawk). If it has a white rump-patch at the base of its tail, similar to a northern harrier, a tail with a broad black band at the tip, and black patches at the "wrist" or bend of the wings, you can feel confident of your identification of a rough-legged hawk. If you see it hover while hunting, you have further confirmation. When these hawks remain in an area and their numbers increase, it is an excellent indicator that local rodent populations are high, particularly those of the meadow vole. Under such conditions, these hawks will continue hunting until increasing snow-depth makes it unprofitable. Then they move on. Ground-roosting short-eared owls often hunt and roost in the same areas that attract the hawks, so anticipate seeing both species. The owls are crepuscular, so they may even be seen foraging in the daytime.

Prior to the snow, an occasional yellow-bellied marmot or least chipmunk may be seen belatedly storing winter food, each in a different place. The marmot stores food around his waist, while the chipmunk stores food in caches that he may relocate, when arousing from a lethargic or torpid state, a condition where breathing, pulse rate, and body temperature are only slightly depressed. This is in contrast to hibernation of the ground squirrel whose body temperature drops from 97 degrees to near freezing (39 degrees). This is accompanied by a reduction in respiration rate from 100 to about 4 breaths per minute. The heart rate goes from 250 to 10 beats per minute. Once in hibernation, ground squirrels can be picked up and handled without awakening. This condition of torpor has advantages in surviving through long, cold winters. On the other hand, it makes them quite vulnerable to active weasels and hungry badgers.

Badger Tracks and Diggings

Bird and mammal activities are now very closely related to daily weather conditions. Along with or following a snow storm, large bands of elk migrate quickly, often at night, into the National Elk Refuge and other smaller wintering areas. Their numbers will build up to about 8,000, currently an appropriate number for the limited winter range. A major storm usually coincides with the height of the fall elk migration. The same storm may now start large flocks of sage grouse flying to wintering sites or encourage the grizzlies to enter their winter dens, now fully excavated and lined with a bed of conifer boughs.

IN THE NATIONAL Elk Refuge the elk will be fed as needed, depending upon the length and severity of the winter. The optimum size of the wintering population is around seven to eight thousand animals. Hunting is the principal means of population control.

In Jackson Hole, pronghorns put on a disappearing act; one day they are here, the next they are gone. By way of the Gros Ventre watershed they travel to lightly covered or snow-free sagebrush areas around Farson, Wyoming. The Jackson Hole

Bison

bison herd that has been roaming Jackson Hole in summer, now moves into the elk refuge to compete with elk for winter range and food. The optimum size of this wintering herd is about one hundred animals. It is small in comparison to the thousands in the Yellowstone Park herd, but is growing steadily. Long-range management for these animals is confronted with the problem of over-population, human encroachment, and subsequent population reduction.

Bison wandering into developed areas can destroy shrubbery and remove bark from small landscaping trees in a matter of minutes. The bison have an affinity for girdling and crushing trees by rubbing against them to get rid of ectoparasites or perhaps merely to scratch their tough hides.

Sage grouse in restless flocks start leaving the valley, some flying into Idaho by way of the Snake River Canyon. Others remain to tough out the winter in wind-swept locales such as slopes on the National Elk Refuge, Uhl Hill, and other areas where sagebrush, their principal food, is not completely covered by snow. Ruffed grouse remain where they have a food supply of aspen and cottonwood buds. Silhouetted against the sky when feeding, they would be easy prey for large raptors, were many present.

Trumpeter Swans

Trumpeter swan numbers vary from place to place and time to time, depending on open water and ice conditions. These large birds need a long water-runway when taking off and are sometimes trapped on small, still water ponds or lakes when plummeting temperatures suddenly turn their water habitat to ice. On one such occasion temperatures dropped from around 20 degrees in the evening to 20 degrees below zero at dawn. As sometimes happens, the transition from water to ice was so rapid that the swans were trapped, unable to take off. They appeared to be frozen into the ice. Motionless, their heads tucked back under their wings, they looked like snow-covered clumps of grass as they awaited the approach of the moving water line advancing slowly toward them—this controlled by the rising sun. When the day temperatures rose, the swans raised their heads, then flapped their wings and waited. They seemed calm and unconcerned, though the situation was one where you might expect panic to reign. Perhaps it would have, had a coyote or a golden eagle appeared before they were free. Though such events are not frequent, they do occur. The swans' behavior under such conditions seemed to reflect an admirable evolutionary adaptation to these extreme changes in weather. The conditions, though unusual, are still characteristic of the climate of the Greater Yellowstone Ecosystem.

The weasels' and snowshoe hares' winter coats are now white. The long-tailed weasel has become an ermine, and the black tip of his tail is about all that makes him visible, in motion or at rest. Delayed snow-cover plays havoc with his winter camouflage— a situation where changes as expressed over time by climate, fail to coincide with local or yearly variations in weather, such as early or late snow storms. Storms that move the elk also initiate the downward movement of bighorns from snow-covered alpine meadows—the zone above timberline. Big buck mule deer are still keeping close tabs on their harems in protected areas where they are undisturbed by hunters.

*Within the spruce-fir zone, snow blankets
the ecosystem. The brown big sagebrush seed stalks
are still protruding. The red, yellow, and silver
willow shoots are not yet covered. The gray-brown
trunks and limbs of the deciduous trees are less
conspicuous than the dark green-needled foliage
of the conifers. Southward bird migration is
largely over. Most animals are now where they
will remain throughout the winter.
Plant life is dormant.*

SOME ELK, LED BY an experienced cow or a large-racked bull, singly or in small groups, may still be on the last stages of their migration down from higher summer and fall ranges. Grizzly and black bears are all in hibernation, as are the smaller mammals: least chipmunks, Uinta ground squirrels, western jumping mice, yellow-bellied marmots, and golden-mantled ground squirrels. These are the segments of the mammal population that will sleep throughout the long winter, relatively secure in their hibernation dens. They will make no tracks.

Most summer residents that leave the Greater Yellowstone area for the winter are gone. This includes most great blue herons, sandhill cranes, white pelicans, blue-winged and cinnamon teals, as well as immature great horned owls, young ravens, immature crows, and young of all the hawks. Birds now present, such as mallards, common goldeneye ducks or "whistlers," northern pin-tails, American wigeons, buffleheads, black-billed magpies, Steller's jays, black-capped chickadees, mountain chickadees, and those still showing up, will be winter residents (Tables II & IX). Some, like snow buntings, come from the north in flocks, while others, like northern shrikes, arrive singly. The pine and evening grosbeaks arrive in small groups. Gray and Steller's jays, Clark's

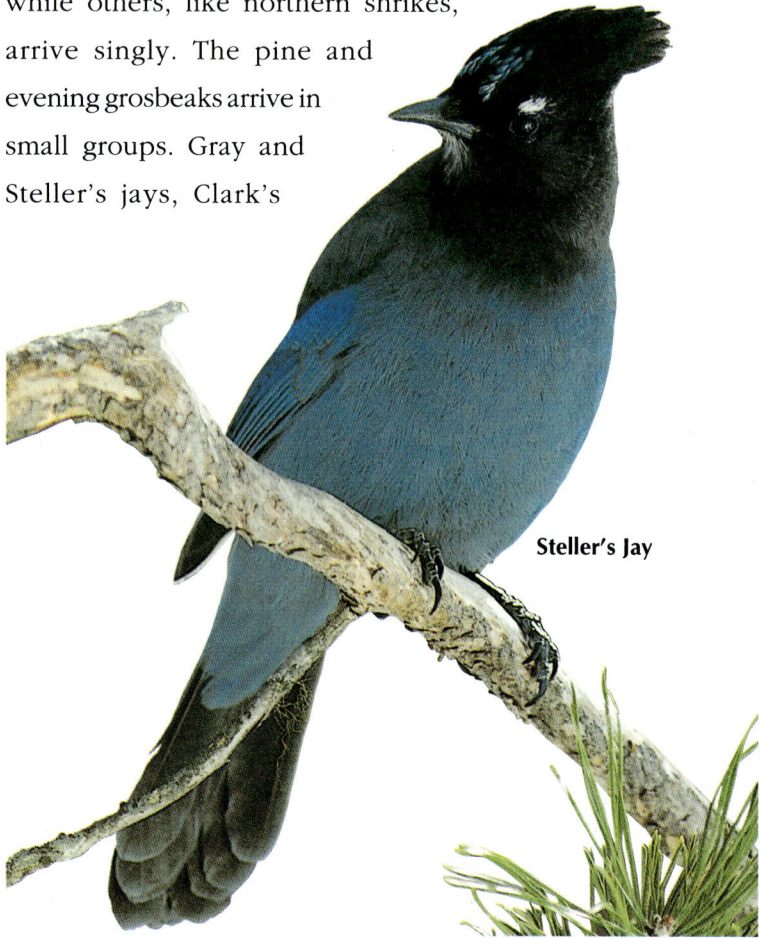

Steller's Jay

MICHAEL S. SAMPLE

160

nutcrackers, mountain chickadees, red-breasted nuthatches, and downy and hairy woodpeckers appear to move up and down in a vertical migration, moving higher or lower as temperatures change. The Jackson Hole, Wyoming, Christmas bird counts (1970-1990) give a representative listing of winter birds, many of which you might expect to see in winter throughout most of the ecosystem. (Table IX).

Snow and wintry conditions generally prevail, but the shortest day of winter is still a month away. Whitefish spawning is over, but fishing for this species continues in Grand Teton National Park throughout the winter. The fish are found in the head and tails of the large and deep pools. If you can get an artificial nymph to the bottom, you can catch whitefish even when slush ice is moving slowly or clogging channels. If it's a case of getting a meal, turn over water-covered rocks along the river's edge and get a live stonefly nymph or helgramite for bait.

*Trumpeter swans are still present in considerable
numbers as are Canada geese, mallards, goldeneyes
(both Barrow's and common), American dippers,
and common and hooded mergansers. Most ponds
and sloughs of still water are frozen, causing
movement of waterfowl to the faster currents of
the Snake River, the year-round habitat of the
American dipper, a small, gray, wren-like bird
that walks on the stream bottom to feed,
even in winter.*

THE BEAVER'S WINTER CACHE of willow and cottonwood
limbs are iced in place in deep water close to the beaver's lodge.
Some bald eagles still patrol sections of the Snake and Yellowstone rivers looking for fish or carrion and will do so throughout
the winter where open water permits. A few golden eagles may
be seen hunting the open country singly or in pairs. Teamed up,
they are far more effective hunters than when foraging singly.
Using a cooperative hunting technique, one bird flying high and
behind, the other one low and ahead, they can and do take prey
as large as mule deer, usually fawns-of-the-year, animals weak-
ened through starvation, or those bogged down in deep snow.

Clark's nutcrackers and gray and Steller's jays are more often

Snow-covered Sage

heard and observed having moved down from higher elevations—part of the altitudinal migration occurring simultaneously
with the latitudinal movements of birds already mentioned.

At noon on sunny days, a few midges will be active on the
snow at the water's edge—a good sign that the whitefish will
feed. The dried stalks and seed heads of sagebrush and bull and
musk thistle, along with those of green gentian, cow parsnip,
loveroot, and timothy, still protrude above the accumulating snow.
Beneath the snow some rose hips and a scattering of silverberries
continue to adhere to bushes, a potential winter meal for wildlife.
Plant or plant related phenological events are now suspended.
The annual cycle will be renewed and continued when warmer
temperatures and increased light start the aspen and cottonwood
buds swelling.

Gardner River

*Snow covers the ground, most summer bird
residents are gone, and many winter migrants and
residents have appeared. Tracks in the snow
replace direct observation as a means of
determining the presence and activities of wildlife.
Cross-country skiing or snowshoeing, rather than
hiking, provides the mobility needed to travel,
track, and observe.*

TRACKS REVEAL THAT the mule deer have moved from higher
country down to the Snake, Buffalo, Gros Ventre, and Grays river
bottoms or to the wind swept ridges. In Jackson Hole, bighorn
sheep have traveled down and may be seen along the Gros Ventre
River near the Red Hills or in the vicinity of Stinking Springs, close
to the Hoback River. At Whiskey Mountain, near Dubois, Wyoming, the largest bighorn herd in the country may be seen. If
persistent and lucky, you may see and photograph a battle between two large rams. In Yellowstone National Park the bighorns
have left the Mount Washburn area to winter in the vicinity of
Mammoth, Wyoming, and Gardiner, Montana. Moose that earlier
trudged through powder snow to browse on the nourishing green
leaf-buds of the bitterbrush now feed on and remain among the
willows of the Snake, Hoback, and Buffalo river bottoms. The

Elk

deepening, wind-packed snow discourages long foraging treks.

Though the grizzlies and black bears mate in June and July, there is a delayed implantation of the fertilized egg in the wall of the uterus and subsequent delayed development of the blasto-cyst until after the bears have entered their dens. Other mammals with a delay between conception and development of the embryo include martens, ermine, long-tailed weasels, minks, wolverine, spotted skunks, badgers, and river otters (Table VII). The birth of young grizzlies (from one to four) occurs about January or February, the young being born helpless, hairless, sightless, and weighing only about twelve to eighteen ounces. Now, in dens covered by deep snow, black and grizzly bears sleep through the long winters of the Greater Yellowstone area without eating, drinking, defecating, or urinating. During this

166

period of hibernation the bear's body temperature drops only slightly (4 to 7 degrees) from their summer temperature of 101 degrees. Their heart rate may go as low as eight beats per minute, and respiration, twelve breaths per minute. The larger the hibernating animal, the lower the metabolic rate. Large animals, such as grizzlies, can fast longer than smaller ones without modification in metabolic level. A hibernating grizzly bear with normal fat reserves can fast for six months with only a slight reduction in body temperature and metabolic rate. This is impossible for small hibernators like ground squirrels, thus the need for a more drastic drop in metabolic rate. The result of such a drop is a more torpid condition for the ground squirrels. Hibernating bears can be readily aroused; ground squirrels cannot.

The tiny tracks of the deermouse in fresh snow are joined by those of the weasel that soon disappear down a tunnel in the snow to emerge ahead. The imprint of large wings, tail, and claws suggest that a great horned owl struck but missed his prey. Ruffed grouse roosting in snow caves of their own fashioning appear well protected from the storms and cold, and safer from maurading martens than they would be roosting on branches of some large Douglas fir—a favorite roost site before snow arrives.

Ravens are foraging, apparently efficiently, in all kinds of weather, even at 60 degrees below zero. Singly, in pairs, or in congregations, they feed on the carcasses of winter or road-killed animals. In winter, toward dusk, some ravens fly in flocks to communal roosts. Crows are largely absent, most having left the Teton-Yellowstone area at about the time of the first snow storms, approximately the same time that young great horned owls migrate to lower and more clement winter ranges.

The non-hibernators are active and leave their tracks, a tell-tale sign in the snow. They include both predator and prey species. The predators are constantly in search of prey in a wintry environment where they must regularly obtain food or they will perish. Some of the prey species available to the collective predator population include deer mice, meadow voles, pocket gophers, bushy-tailed wood rats, snowshoe hares, jack rabbits, red squirrels, flying squirrels, pikas, beavers, shrews, and even some of the hibernators, such as ground squirrels (vulnerable to the badger). Bighorn sheep, elk, deer, and porcupines may occasionally be taken by a mountain lion. Other predators active in winter, whose tracks and scats you may see, include weasels, martens, minks, otters, skunks, badgers, coyotes, lynx, bobcats, and possibly, but very unlikely, the wolverine or the gray wolf.

Tracks in the snow may be the only indication that a mountain lion is in the vicinity. Following the tracks may lead to an elk killed and largely consumed by the big cat or to lion scrapings—droppings covered with earth, grass, or humus. These signs, along with track size and pattern, the large size of the prey species taken, and the apparent ease with which it has been pulled and dragged about, may further confirm the presence and activity of a rare mountain lion. Evidence of its presence is often indirect with no sightings to thrill the observer. The nearby remains of a porcupine turned inside out, the dried skin still armed with quills, is further confirmation of lion activity and makes one speculate

on how the lion man-
ages to kill and consume
this well-armed animal
without suffering a face
full of barbed quills.

In the coniferous
timber of pine, spruce,
and fir, foraging martens
create breaks in their trail

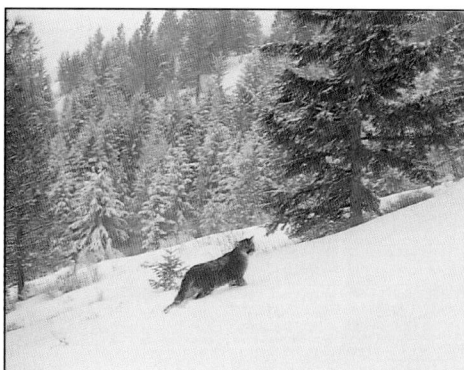

Mountain Lion

as they vacillate between traveling through the trees or on the
snow. Their tracks may merge with those of a red squirrel or
chickaree returning from its midden, a winter cache of cones and
seeds at the base of a large evergreen tree.

Where in summer you have seen ground squirrel burrows and
numerous scampering rodents, you may in winter see circular
mounds and cones of fresh earth thrown up by badgers digging
down to locate, kill, and consume the soundly sleeping ground
squirrels. When freshly dug, these earthen cones stand out in
sharp contrast to the surrounding snow. The tread-like tracks
leading to and from the earth piles look as though they were
made by a toy bulldozer. At times the mounds are so numerous
they make one wonder whether the squirrel colony will survive
or how many will see the light of a spring day?

Another mustelid, or fur-bearing mammal, of the weasel family,
which is active and perhaps more readily viewed in winter than
in summer, is the river otter, undulating in porpoise fashion as he
swims against the current. In the water he leaves no trail, but on

Red Squirrel

land his tracks, ice slides, and fish scale and bone droppings, tell of his past presence and give promise of a future meeting.

There is now sufficient snow to initiate sleigh rides into the Elk Refuge. Bundled up in warm clothing, visitors may obtain close-up views of elk and unique photo opportunities. Similarly, snow-mobile and snow-coach trips into Yellowstone provide addi-tional opportunities to observe wildlife coping with winters of deep snow and low temperatures—this epitomized by a cloud of erupting snow through which is glimpsed a rare lynx in pursuit of a nearly invisible snowshoe hare. Year-round resident great horned owls, their hormone production influenced by increasing light, hoot and call to one another, thus initiating another nesting cycle for which they are the forerunners. By imitating and return-ing the calls, you may lure the hooter close enough for a good identifying look.

The wonder of the world, the beauty and
the power, the shapes of things, their
colours, lights, and shades; these I saw.
Look ye also while life lasts.

Originally from an old gravestone
in Cumberland, England.

TABLES

TABLE I
PLANTS IN THE ECOSYSTEM

Alfalfa .... *Medicago sativa*

American Bistort .... *Polygonum bistortoides*

Anemone .... *Anemone globosa*

Arnica .... *Arnica cordifolia*

Arrowleaf Balsamroot .... *Balsamorhiza sagittata*

Arrowleaf Groundsel .... *Senecio triangularis*

Ballhead Sandwort .... *Arenaria congesta*

Baneberry .... *Actaea arguta*

Bearberry (or Kinnikinnick) .... *Arctostaphylos uva-ursi*

Bedstraw .... *Galium boreale*

Beggarticks .... *Bidens cernua*

Big Sagebrush .... *Artemisia tridentata*

Big Whortleberry (or Huckleberry) ....*Vaccinium mambranaceum*

Bitterbrush .... *Purshia tridentata*

Bittercress .... *Cardamine breweri*

Bitterroot .... *Lewisia rediviva*

Black Currant .... *Ribes lacustre*

Black Morel .... *Morchella angusticeps*

Black Twinberry .... *Lonicera involucrata*

Blackbead Elder .... *Sambucus melanocarpa*

Blue Camas .... *Camassia quamash*

Blue Flax .... *Linum lewisii*

Blue Penstemon .... *Penstemon cyaneus*

Blue Violet .... *Viola adunca*

Bluebonnet (or Silky Lupine) ..... *Lupinus sericeus*

Blue-flowered Lettuce .... *Lactuca pulchella*

Blue-lips (or Blue-eyed Mary) .... *Collinsia parviflora*

Bristle Thistle .... *Carduus nutans*

Broadleaf (or Black) Cottonwood .... *Populus trichocarpa*

Broadleaf Fireweed .... *Epilobium latifolium*

Buckwheat .... *Eriogonum heracleoides*

Bull Thistle .... *Cirsium vulgare*

Burdock .... *Arctium minus*

Butterweed Groundsel .... *Senecio serra*

Butter-and-Eggs .... *Linaria dalmatica*

Canada Thistle .... *Cirsium arvense*

Chokecherry .... *Prunus melanocarpa*

Cocklebur .... *Xanthium strumarium*

Columbia Monkshood .... *Aconitum columbianum*

Columbine (or Blue Columbine) .... *Aquilegia coerulea*

Cow Parsnip .... *Heracleum sphondylium*

Crazyweeds .... *Oxytropis besseyi*

Curlydock .... *Rumex crispus*

Dalmation Toadflax .... *Linaria dalmatica*

Dandelion .... *Taraxacum officinale*

Death Camas .... *Zigadenus paniculatus*

Desert-parsley .... *Lomatium foeniculaceum*

Dogbane .... *Apocynum androsaemifolium*

Douglas Fir .... *Pseudotsuga menziesii*

Dyers Woad .... *Isatis tinctoria*

Early Paintbrush .... *Castilleja chromosa*

Elderberry .... *Sambucus coerulea*

Elephanthead .... *Pedicularis groenlandica*

Elk Sedge .... *Carex geyeri*

Elk Thistle .... *Cirsium scariosum*

Engelmann Aster .... *Aster engelmannii*

Evening Primrose .... *Oenothera caespitosa*

Fairybells .... *Disporum trachycarpum*

Fairyslipper .... *Calypso bulbosa*

False Forget-me-not .... *Hackelia floribunda*

False Huckleberry (Rusty Menziesia or Rusty Leaf) .... *Menziesia furruginea*

False Solomonseal .... *Smilacina racemosum*

Fernleaf .... *Pedicularis bracteosa*

Fever Few .... *Chrysanthemum parthenium*

Fireweed .... *Epilobium angustifolium*

Forget-me-not .... *Myosotis laxa*

Foxtail Barley .... *Hordeum jubatum*

Fringed Sagebrush .... *Artemisia frigida*

Giant Hyssop .... *Agastache urticifolia*

Glacier Lily (or Dogtooth Violet) .... *Erythronium grandiflorum*

Golden Aster .... *Heterotheca villosa*

Golden Corydalis (or Golden Smoke) .... *Corydalis aurea*

Golden Currant .... *Ribes aureum*

Goldeneye .... *Viguiera multiflora*

Goldenrod .... *Solidago elongata*

Golden Wooley Aster .... *Chrysopsis villosa*
Gooseberry .... *Ribes* sp.
Green Gentian .... *Frasera speciosa*
Gromwell .... *Lithospermum incisum*
Grouse Whortleberry .... *Vaccinium scoparium*
Gumweed .... *Grindelia squarrosa*
Harebell .... *Campanula rotundifolia*
Hawksbeard .... *Crepis acuminata*
Hawkweed .... *Hieracium albertinum*
Hawthorne .... *Crataegus rivularis*
Henbane .... *Hyoscyamus niger*
Holly-grape (or Oregon Grape) .... *Mahonia repens*
Hop-trefoil .... *Trifolium campestre*
Hornemann Willowweed .... *Epilobium hornemannii*
Houndstongue .... *Cynoglossum officinale*
Indian (or Scarlet) Paintbrush .. *Castilleja miniata*
Indian Potato .... *Orogenia linearifolia*
Jacob's Ladder .... *Polemonium pulcherrimum*
Ladies Tresses .... *Spiranthes romanzoffiana*
Leafy Spurge .... *Euphorbia esula*
Leopard Lily .... *Lilium pardalinum*
Lewisia .... *Lewisia pygmaea*
Limber Pine .... *Pinus flexilis*
Little Sunflower .... *Helianthella uniflora*
Locoweed (or Pursh Milkvetch) .... *Astragalus purshii*
Lodgepole Lupine .... *Lupinus parviflorus*
Lodgepole Pine .... *Pinus contorta*
Long-leafed Phlox .... *Phlox longifolia*
Long-plumed Avens (or Prairie Smoke) ..... *Geum triflorum*
Loveroot .... *Ligusticum filicinum*
Matchbrush .... *Gutierrezia sarothrae*
Morel .... *Morchella*
Mountain Alder .... *Alnus incana*
Mountain Ash .... *Sorbus scopulina*
Mountain Bluebells .... *Mertensia viridis*
Mountain Dandelion .... *Agoseris glauca*
Mountain Death Camas .... *Zigadenus elegans*
Mountain Hollyhock (Mountain Globemallow or Wild Hollyhock) .... *Iliamna rivularis*
Mules-ears .... *Wyethia amplexicaulis*
Mullein .... *Verbascum thapsus*

Narrowleaf Cottonwood ..... *Populus angustifolia*
Nelson's Larkspur .... *Delphinium nelsoni*
Onion (or Melica) Grass .... *Melica bulbosa*
Ox-eye Daisy .... *Chrysanthemum leucanthemum*
Oysterplant (or Meadow Salsifly) .... *Tragopogon pratensis*
Parrots-beak .... *Pedicularis racemosa*
Pearly Everlasting .... *Anaphalis margaritacea*
Pinedrops .... *Pterospora andromedea*
Pink Pyrola .... *pyrola asarifolia*
Pink Spirea .... *Spiraea douglasii*
Pleated Gentian .... *Gentiana affinis*
Prickly Currant .... *Ribes lacustre*
Prickly Lettuce .... *Latuca serriola*
Prince's Pine (or Wintergreen) .... *Chimaphila umbellata*
Puffball .... *Calvatia*
Quaking Aspen .... *Populus tremuloides*
Queencup .... *Clintonia uniflora*
Rabbit-brush .... *Chrysothamnus nauseosus*
Red Monkeyflower .... *Mimulus lewisii*
Red Twinberry .... *Lonicera utahensis*
Red-osier Dogwood .... *Cornus stolonifera*
River Hawthorn .... *Crataegus rivularis*
Rocky Mountain Ash .... *Sorbus scopulina*
Rocky Mountain Juniper .... *Juniperus scopulorum*
Rocky Mountain Maple .... *Acer glabrum*
Roundstem Bulrush .... *Scirpus acutus*
Rushpink .... *Lygodesmia grandiflora*
Russet Buffaloberry .... *Shepherdia canadensis*
Rusty Menziesia .... *Menziesia ferruginea*
Sagebrush .... *Artemisia tridentata*
Sagebrush Buttercup ..... *Ranunculus glaberrimus*
Scarlet Gilia .... *Gilia aggregata*
Sego (or Mariposa) Lily .... *Calochortus nuttallii*
Serviceberry .... *Amelanchier alnifolia*
Shooting Star .... *Dodecatheon pauciflorum*
Shore Buttercup .... *Ranunculus cymbalaria*
Showy Cinquefoil .... *Potentilla gracilis*
Showy Daisy .... *Erigeron speciosus*
Shrubby Cinquefoil .... *Pentaphylloides floribunda*
Silky Phacelia .... *Phacelia sericea*
Silver Sagebrush .... *Artemisia cana*
Silverberry .... *Eleagnus commutata*

174

Silverweed Cinquefoil
(or Five Fingers) .... *Potentilla anserina*

Snowberry .... *Symphoricarpos oreophilos*

Snowbrush .... *Ceanothus velutinus*

Sow Thistle .... *Sonchus arvensis*

Spirea .... *Spiraea splendens*

Sponge Morel .... *Morchella esculenta*

Spotted Coralroot .... *Corallorhiza maculata*

Spotted Knapweed .... *Centaurea maculosa*

Spring Beauty .... *Claytonia lanceolata*

Squawbush .... *Rhus trilobata*

Star Flower .... *Lithophragma parviflora*

Steershead .... *Dicentra uniflora*

Stemless Goldenweed .... *Haplopappus acaulis*

Stickseed .... *Hackelia floribunda*

Sticky Geranium .... *Geranium viscosissimum*

Stinging Nettle .... *Urtica dioica*

Stonecrop .... *Sedum stenopetalum*

Subalpine Fir .... *Abies lasiocarpa*

Sugarbowl .... *Clematis hirsutissima*

Sulphur Cinquefoil .... *Potentilla recta*

Swamp-laurel .... *Kalmia polifolia*

Sweet Vetch .... *Hedysarum occidentale*

Tall Larkspur .... *Delphinium occidentale*

Tansy .... *Tanacetum vulgare*

Thickstem Aster .... *Aster integrifolius*

Thimbleberry .... *Rubus parviflorus*

Timothy .... *Phleum pratense*

Tobacco Root (or Valeriana) .... *Valerian dioica*

Twinberry Honeysuckle ...... *Lonicera involucrata*

Twisted-stalk .... *Streptopus amplexifolius*

Two-grooved Milkvetch ...... *Astragalus bisulcatus*

Water Buttercup .... *Ranunculus aquatilis*

Water Groundsel .... *Senecio hydrophilus*

Water Ladysthumb .... *Polygonum amphibium*

Water Parsnip .... *Sium suave*

Water Speedwell ...... *Veronica anagallis-aquatica*

Waterleaf .... *Hydrophyllum capitatum*

Western Baneberry .... *Actaea rubra*

Western Coneflower .... *Rudbeckia occidentalis*

Western Fringed Gentian .... *Gentiana thermalis*

Western Meadow Rue .... *Thalictrum occidentale*

Western Polemonium .... *Polemonium occidentale*

White Bog-orchid .... *Habenaria dilatata*

White Clematis .... *Clematis ligusticifolia*

White Phlox .... *Phlox multiflora*

White Spirea .... *Spiraea betulifolia*

White Wyethia .... *Wyethia helianthoides*

Whitebark Pine .... *Pinus albicaulis*

Whitestem Gooseberry .... *Ribes inerme*

Whorled Buckwheat (or Umbrella
Plant) .... *Eriogonum Heracleoides*

Wild Chives .... *Allium schoenoprasum*

Wild Hyacinth .... *Triteleia grandiflora*

Wild Licorice .... *Glycyrrhiza lepidota*

Wild (or Nodding) Onion .... *Allium cernuum*

Wild Red Raspberry .... *Rubus idaeus*

Wild Rose .... *Rosa woodsii*

Willow Family .... *Salicaceae*

Wintergreen .... *Chimaphila umbellatus*

Woodland Strawberry .... *Fragaria vesca*

Woolly Yellow Daisy .... *Eriophyllum lanatum*

Wyeth Biscuitroot .... *Lomatium ambiguum*

Yampa .... *Perideridia gairdneri*

Yarrow .... *Achillea lanulosa*

Yellowbell (or Yellow Fritillary) .... *Fritillaria pudica*

Yellow Evening Primrose .... *Oenothera villosa*

Yellow Monkeyflower .... *Mimulus guttatus*

Yellow Pondlily .... *Nuphar polysepalum*

Yellow Sweet Clover .... *Melilotus officinalis*

Yellow Violet .... *Viola nuttallii*

Yellow-flowered Groundsel .... *Senecio integerrimus*

TABLE II
ECOSYSTEM BREEDING BIRDS

American Avocet .... *Recurvirostra americana*
American Bittern .... *Botaurus lentiginosus*
American Coot .... *Fulica americana*
American Crow .... *Corvus brachyrhynchos*
American Dipper .... *Cinclus mexicanus*
American Goldfinch .... *Carduelis tristis*
American Kestrel .... *Falco sparverius*
American Pipit .... *Anthus spinoletta*
American Robin .... *Turdus migratorius*
American White Pelican .... *Pelecanus erythrorhynchos*
American Wigeon (or Baldpate) .... *Anas americana*
Bald Eagle .... *Haliaeetus leucocephalus*
Bank Swallow .... *Riparia riparia*
Barn Swallow .... *Hirundo rustica*
Barrow's Goldeneye .... *Bucephala islandica*
Belted Kingfisher .... *Megaceryle alcyon*
Black Tern .... *Chlidonias niger*
Black-backed Woodpecker ...... *Picoides arcticus*
Black-billed Magpie .... *Pica pica*
Black-capped Chickadee .... *Parus atricapillus*
Black-headed Grosbeak .... *Pheucticus melanocephalus*
Blue Grouse .... *Dendragapus obscurus*
Blue-winged Teal .... *Anas discors*
Boreal Owl .... *Aegolius funereus*
Brewer's Blackbird .... *Euphagus cyanocephalus*
Brewer's Sparrow .... *Spizella breweri*
Broad-tailed Hummingbird .... *Selasphorus platycercus*
Brown Creeper .... *Certhia familiaris*
Brown-headed Cowbird .... *Molothrus ater*
Bufflehead .... *Bucephala albeola*
California Gull .... *Larus californicus*
Calliope Hummingbird .... *Stellula calliope*
Canada Goose .... *Branta canadensis*
Canvasback .... *Aythya valisineria*
Cassin's Finch .... *Carpodacus cassinii*
Chipping Sparrow .... *Spizella passerina*
Cinnamon Teal .... *Anas cyanoptera*

Clark's Nutcracker .... *Nucifraga columbiana*
Clay-colored Sparrow .... *Spizella pallida*
Cliff Swallow .... *Petrocheldon pyrrhonaota*
Common Loon .... *Gavia immer*
Common Merganser .... *Mergus merganser*
Common Nighthawk .... *Chordeiles minor*
Common Raven .... *Corvus corax*
Common Snipe .... *Capella gallinago*
Common Yellowthroat .... *Geothlypis trichas*
Cooper's Hawk .... *Accipiter cooperii*
Cordilleran Flycatcher .... *Empidonax difficilis*
Downy Woodpecker .... *Picoides pubescens*
Dusky Flycatcher .... *Empidonax oberholseri*
European Starling .... *Sturnus vulgaris*
Evening Grosbeak .... *Coccothraustes vesperinus*
Ferruginous Hawk .... *Buteo regalis*
Fox Sparrow .... *Passerella iliaca*
Gadwall .... *Anas strepera*
Golden Eagle .... *Aquila chrysaetos*
Gray Catbird .... *Dumetella carolinensis*
Gray Jay .... *Perisoreus canadensis*
Gray Partridge .... *Perdix perdix*
Great Blue Heron .... *Ardea herodias*
Great Gray Owl .... *Strix nebulosa*
Great Horned Owl .... *Bubo virginianus*
Green-tailed Towhee .... *Pipilo chlorurus*
Green-winged Teal .... *Anas crecca*
Hairy Woodpecker .... *Picoides villosus*
Harlequin Duck .... *Histrionicus histrionicus*
Hermit Thrush .... *Catharus guttatus*
Horned Lark .... *Eremophila alpestris*
House Sparrow .... *Passer domesticus*
House Wren .... *Troglodytes aedon*
Killdeer .... *Charadrius vociferus*
Lark Sparrow .... *Chondestes grammacus*
Lazuli Bunting .... *Passerina amoena*
Lesser Scaup .... *Aythya affinis*
Lewis' Woodpecker .... *Melanerpes lewis*
Lincoln's Sparrow .... *Melospiza lincolnii*

176

Long-billed Curlew .... Numenius americanus
Long-eared Owl .... Asio otus
MacGillivray's Warbler .... Oporornis tolmiei
Mallard .... Anas platyrhynchos
Northern Harrier (or Marsh Hawk) .... Circus cyaneus
Marsh Wren .... Cistothorus palustris
Merlin .... Falco columbarius
Mountain Bluebird .... Sialia currucoides
Mountain Chickadee .... Parus gambeli
Mourning Dove .... Zenaida macroura
Northern Flicker .... Colaptes auratus
Northern Goshawk .... Accipiter gentilis
Northern Oriole .... Icterus galbula
Northern Pintail .... Anas acuta
Northern Pygmy-Owl .... Glaucidium gnoma
Northern Rough-winged Swallow .... Stelgidoppteryx ruficollis
Northern Saw-whet Owl .... Aegolius acadicus
Northern Shoveler .... Anas clypeata
Olive-sided Flycatcher .... Nuttallornis borealis
Orange-crowned Warbler .... Vermivora celata
Oregon (or Pink-sided) Junco .... Junco oreganus
Osprey .... Pandion haliaetus
Peregrine Falcon .... Falco peregrinus
Pied-billed Grebe .... Podilymbus podiceps
Pine Siskin .... Carduelis pinus
Prairie Falcon .... Falco mexicanus
Red Crossbill .... Loxia curvirostra
Redhead .... Aythya americana
Red-breasted Nuthatch .... Sitta canadensis
Red-naped Sapsucker .... Sphyrapicus nuchalis
Red-tailed Hawk .... Buteo jamaicensis
Red-winged Blackbird .... Agelaius phoeniceus
Ring-necked Duck .... Aythya collaris
Ring-necked Pheasant .... Phasianus colchicus
Rock Wren .... Salpinctes obsoletus
Ruby-crowned Kinglet .... Regulus calendula
Ruddy Duck .... Oxyura jamaicensis
Ruffed Grouse .... Bonasa umbellus
Rufous Hummingbird .... Selasphorus rufus
Sage Grouse .... Centrocercus urophasianus
Sage Sparrow .... Amphispiza belli

Sage Thrasher .... Oreoscoptes montanus
Sandhill Crane .... Grus canadensis
Savannah Sparrow .... Passerculus sandwichensis
Sharp-shinned Hawk .... Accipiter striatus
Sharp-tailed Grouse .... Pedioecetes phasianellus
Short-eared Owl .... Asio flammeus
Song Sparrow .... Melospiza melodia
Sora .... Porzana carolina
Spotted Sandpiper .... Actitis macularia
Steller's Jay .... Cyanocitta stelleri
Swainson's Hawk .... Buteo swainsoni
Swainson's Thrush .... Catharus ustulatus
Three-toed Woodpecker ..... Picoides tridactylus
Townsend's Solitaire .... Myadestes townsendi
Tree Swallow .... Iridoprocne bicolor
Trumpeter Swan .... Cygnus buccinator
Turkey vulture .... Cathartes aura
Vesper Sparrow .... Pooecetes gramineus
Violet-green Swallow .... Tachycineta thalassina
Virginia Rail .... Rallus limicola
Warbling Vireo .... Vireo gilvus
Western Grebe .... Aechmophorus occidentalis
Western Kingbird .... Tyrannus verticalis
Western Meadowlark .... Sturnella neglecta
Western Screech Owl .... Otus kennicotti
Western Tanager .... Piranga ludoviciana
Western Wood-Pewee .... Contopus sordidulus
White-breasted Nuthatch .... Sitta carolinensis
White-crowned Sparrow .... Zonotrichia leucophrys
White-throated Swift .... Aeronautes saxatalis
Willet .... Catoptrophorus semipalmatus
Williamson's Sapsucker .... Sphyrapicus thyroideus
Willow Flycatcher .... Empidonax traillii
Wilson's Phalarope .... Phalaropus tricolor
Yellow Warbler .... Dendroica petechia
Yellow-headed Blackbird .... Xanthocephalus xanthocephalus
Yellow-rumped Warbler .... Dendroica coronata

TABLE III
BIRDS PASSING THROUGH THE ECOSYSTEM

Hooded Merganser .... *Lophodytes cucullatus*	Red-breasted Merganser .... *Mergus serrator*
House Finch .... *Carpodacus mexicanus*	Rough-legged Hawk .... *Buteo lagopus*
Lesser Yellowlegs .... *Tringa Flauipes*	Snow Goose .... *Chen caerulescens*
Northern Shrike .... *Lanius excubitor*	Whooping Crane .... *Grus americana*
Pine Grosbeak .... *Pinicola enucleator*	Wood Duck .... *Aix sponsa*
Purple Grackle .... *Quiscalus quiscula*	

TABLE IV
MAMMALS OF THE ECOSYSTEM

Badger .... *Taxidea taxus*	Moose .... *Alces alces*
Beaver .... *Castor canadensis*	Mountain Lion .... *Felis concolor*
Bighorn Sheep .... *Ovis canadensis*	Mule Deer .... *Odocoileus hemionus*
Bison .... *Bison bison*	Muskrat .... *Ondatra zibethicus*
Black Bear .... *Ursus americanus*	Northern Flying Squirrel .... *Glaucomys sabrinus*
Bobcat .... *Felis rufus*	Northern Pocket Gopher ... *Thomomys talpoides*
Bushy-tailed Woodrat .... *Neotoma cinerea*	Pika .... *Ochotona princeps*
Coyote .... *Canis latrans*	Porcupine .... *Erethizon dorsatum*
Deer Mouse .... *Peromyscus maniculatus*	Pronghorn .... *Antilocapra americana*
Elk .... *Cervus elaphus*	Red Fox .... *Vulpes vulpes*
Ermine .... *Mustela erminea*	Red Squirrel .... *Tamiasciurus hudsonicus*
Golden-mantled Ground Squirrel .... *Spermophilus lateralis*	River Otter .... *Lutra canadensis*
	Shrew .... *Family: Soricidae*
Grizzly Bear .... *Ursus arctos*	Snowshoe Hare .... *Lepus americanus*
Least Chipmunk .... *Tamias minimus*	Striped Skunk .... *Mephitis mephitis*
Least Weasel .... *Mustela nivalis*	Uinta Ground Squirrel ..... *Spermophilus armatus*
Long-tailed Vole .... *Microtus longicaudus*	Western Jumping Mouse .... *Zapus princeps*
Long-tailed Weasel .... *Mustela frenata*	Western Spotted Skunk .... *Spilogale gracilis*
Lynx .... *Felis lynx*	White-footed Mouse ..... *Peromyscus maniculatus*
Marten .... *Martes americana*	White-tailed Deer .... *Odocoileus virginianus*
Meadow Mouse .... *Microtus pennsylvanicus*	White-tailed Jackrabbit .... *Lepus townsendii*
Meadow Vole .... *Microtus pennsylvanicus*	Wolverine .... *Gulo gulo*
Mink .... *Mustela vison*	Yellow-bellied Marmot .... *Marmota flaviventris*

TABLE V
ADDITIONAL SCIENTIFIC NAMES

Brown Trout .... *Salmo trutta*
Cabbage Butterfly .... *Artogeia rapae*
Caddis Fly .... *Trichoptera* sp.
Cecropia Moth .... *Hyalophora cecropia*
Chorus Frog .... *Pseudacris triseriata*
Comma Butterfly .... *Polygonia comma*
Crane Fly .... *Tipula* sp.
Cutthroat Trout .... *Oncorhynchus clarki*
Deer Fly .... *Chrysops* sp.
Dog (or Wood) Tick .... *Dermacentor variabilis*
Dragonfly .... Order: Odonata
Eastern Brook Trout .... *Salvelinus fontinalis fontinalis*
Forest Tent Caterpillar .... *Malacosoma disstria*
Glover's Silk Moth .... *Hyalophora gloveri*
Golden Stonefly .... *Hesperoperla pacifica*
Gray Drake .... *Siphlonurus occidentalis*
Hawk Moth .... Family: Sphingidae
Lake Trout, Mackinaw .... *Salvelinus namaycush*
May Fly .... *Baetis tricaudatus*
Mayfly .... Order: Ephemeroptera

Midge (or Snow Mosquito) .... *Chironomid* sp.
Milbert's Tortoiseshell .... *Aglais milberti*
Mormon Cricket .... *Anabrus simplex*
Mosquito .... *Culicinae* sp.
Mountain Sucker .... *Catostomus platyrhynchus*
Mourning Cloak Butterfly ...... *Nymphalis antiopa*
Musk Thistle Weevil .... *Trichosirocalus horridus*
Painted-lady Butterfly .... *Vanessa cardui*
Red Admiral .... *Vanessa atalanta*
Rocky Mountain Whitefish .... *Prosopium williamsoni*
Salmon Fly .... *Pteronarcys californica*
Sheridan's Hairstreak Butterfly .... *Callophrys sheridanii*
Spruce Budworm .... *Choristoneura fumiferana*
Tiger Salamander .... *Ambystoma tigrinum*
Tiger Swallowtail .... *Papilio glaucus*
Utah Chub (or Squawfish) .... *Gila atraria*
Utah Sucker .... *Catostomus ardens*
Western Swallowtail Butterfly .... *Papilio rutulus*
Yellow Swallowtail Butterfly .... *Papilio nitra*

TABLE VI
BASE AREA METEOROLOGICAL TABLE

TEMP. AND PRECIPITATION	JAN	FEB	MAR	APR	MAY	JUN	JUL	AUG	SEP	OCT	NOV	DEC
Avg. high temp. (°F)	27	32	38	48	59	69	79	78	68	54	38	25
Avg. low temp. (°F)	1	6	13	22	31	37	41	38	32	22	14	4
Extreme high temp. (°F)	45	55	61	70	81	88	91	93	88	76	62	48
Extreme low temp. (°F)	-46	-42	-25	-10	9	21	26	23	9	1	-20	-43
Avg. snowfall (inches)	38	20	16	6	4	0	0	0	1	3	28	39
Avg. rainfall (inches)	0	0	0	1	3	2	1	1	1	1	0	0

TABLE VII
MAMMAL REPRODUCTIVE CHART

SPECIES	MATING, BREEDING, RUT	GESTATION (MONTHS)	BIRTH, CALVING, WELPING
Pika	Late winter	1.0	Apr - May
Snowshoe Hare	Mar - Jun	5 wks	Apr - Aug
White-tailed Jackrabbit	Mar - Aug	1.5	Apr - Aug
Least Chipmunk	Mar - May	1.0	May - Jun
Yellow-bellied Marmot	May	1.0	Jun
Uinta Ground Squirrel	Apr - May	1.0	May- Jun
Red Squirrel	Feb - Apr	1.0	Mar - May
Northern Flying Squirrel	Apr - May	1.5	May - Jun
Northern Pocket Gopher	Mar - Apr	2.0	May - Jun
Beaver	Jan - Feb	-	May - Jun
Deer Mouse	Spring - Fall	1.0	Summer - Fall
Bushy-tailed Woodrat	Spring - Summer	1.0	Summer - Fall
Meadow Vole	Year-round	3 wks	Anytime
Muskrat	Apr - May	1.0	May - Jun
Porcupine	Fall	7-8	Spring
Coyote	Mid-Feb	2.0	Mid-Apr
Gray Wolf	Feb - Apr	2.0	Mar - May
Red Fox	Dec - Mar	2.0 (app.)	Feb - Apr
Black Bear	Jun -Jul	7*	Jan - Feb
Grizzly Bear	Jun - Jul	7*	Jan - Feb
Marten	Aug-Sep	9*	Mar - Apr
Ermine	Jul - Aug	9*	Mar - Apr
Long-tailed Weasel	Jul - Aug	9*	Mar - Apr
Mink	Feb - Apr	3.0	Apr - May
Badger	Aug - Sep	9*	Mar - Apr
Western Spotted Skunk	Sep - Oct	6.0	Spring
Striped Skunk	Feb - Mar	2.0	May - Jun
River Otter	Feb - Apr	7 wks*	Nov - May
Mountain Lion	Apr - May	3.0	Jul - Aug
Bobcat	Jan - Jul	2.0	Apr - Sep
Elk	Sep - Oct	8.5	May - Jun
Mule Deer	Oct - Dec	7.0	Jun - Jul
Whlte-tailed Deer	Nov - Feb	6.5	Jun - Jul
Moose	Sep - Oct	8.0	May - Jun
Pronghorn	Aug - Oct	8.0	May - Jun
Bison	Aug - Oct	9.0	May - Jun
Mountain Goat	Nov - Dec	6.0	May - Jun
Bighorn Sheep	Nov - Dec	6.0	May - Jun

*DELAYED IMPLANTATION

TABLE VIII
NESTING RAPTORS

SPECIES	INCUBATION PERIOD WEEKS	NESTLING PERIOD WEEKS	ADULT CONFINED TO NEST WEEKS
Turkey Vulture	6	12	18
Osprey	5	9	14
Bald Eagle	5	11	16
Northern Harrier	4	5	9
Sharp-shinned Hawk	5	4	9
Cooper's Hawk	5	5	10
Northern Goshawk	5	6	11
Swainson's Hawk	5	6	11
Red-tailed Hawk	5	6	11
Ferruginous Hawk	5	7	12
Golden Eagle	6	11	17
American Kestrel	4	4	8
Merlin	4	5	9
Peregrine Falcon	5	6	11
Prairie Falcon	5	6	11
Screech Owl	4	4	8
Great Horned Owl	5	5	10
Great Gray Owl	5	7	12
Long-eared Owl	4	4	8
Short-eared Owl	4	5	9
Boreal Owl	4	5	9
Northern Saw-whet Owl	4	4	8
Northern Pygmy Owl	4	4	8

TABLE IX
JACKSON HOLE, WYOMING
CHRISTMAS BIRD COUNTS 1970 - 1990
Courtesy of the Jackson Hole Bird Club

SPECIES	1970	1974	1978	1982	1986	1990
Great Blue Heron	-	1	CW	1	-	1
Tundra Swan	-	-	-	15	20	2
Trumpeter Swan	17	18	10	54	60	92
Snow Goose*	-	-	CW	-	-	-
Canada Goose	10	71	45	198	105	442
Green-winged Teal	26	65	19	42	21	31
Mallard	96	100	284	414	342	616
Northern Pintail	2	44	17	52	25	8
Blue-winged Teal*	-	-	-	-	-	-
Teal, sp.	-	-	-	-	-	30
Northern Shoveler*	-	-	-	-	-	-
Gadwall	-	2	10	43	20	26
American Wigeon	-	-	1	-	8	1
Redhead*	-	-	-	2	-	-
Ring-necked Duck	2	5	16	-	20	1
Lesser Scaup*	-	-	-	1	2	-
Common Goldeneye	29	17	15	6	38	6
Barrow's Goldeneye	58	7	198	130	122	112
Goldeneye, sp.	-	-	-	-	12	80
Bufflehead	16	16	17	34	12	13
Hooded Merganser	-	-	-	1	4	5
Common Merganser	1	-	35	10	29	12
Ruddy Duck*	-	-	-	-	-	-
Duck, sp.	-	-	-	-	-	-
Bald Eagle	21	?	12	26	20	33
Northern Harrier*	-	1	-	-	-	-
Cooper's Hawk*	-	-	-	-	-	-
Northern Goshawk	-	-	-	1	-	CW
Accipiter, sp.	-	-	-	-	1	-
Swainson's Hawk**	1 *(This is probably a misidentification)*			-	-	-
Red-tailed Hawk	-	-	-	-	1	1

SPECIES	1970	1974	1978	1982	1986	1990
Rough-legged Hawk	1	-	1	4	-	8
Buteo, sp.	-	-	-	-	-	-
Golden Eagle	5	9	1	5	4	3
Merlin	-	-	-	-	-	- -
American Kestrel	-	-	-	-	-	-
Prairie Falcon	-	-	-	-	-	-
Gray Partridge	-	-	-	CW	-	-
Blue Grouse	-	-	1	-	-	-
Ruffed Grouse	-	2	2	5	4	3
Winter Wren*	-	-	-	-	-	-
American Dipper	3	7	33	11	29	14
Golden-crowned Kinglet	-	-	-	-	CW	1
Ruby-crowned Kinglet*	-	-	-	10^	-	
Townsend's Solitaire	1	1	5	3	1	4
American Robin*	-	-	1	1	CW	-
Water Pipit*	-	-	-	-	-	1
Bohemian Waxwing	-	39	8	-	15	206
Cedar Waxwing	-	-	1	-	36	CW
Northern Shrike	1	-	2	2	-	2
Loggerhead Shrike**	-	-	-	-	-	1
European Starling	11	11	68	1	34	1
Rufous-sided Towhee*	-	-	-	-	-	-
American Tree Sparrow	-	2	19	19	-	5
Chipping Sparrow**	-	-	-	-	-	-
Song Sparrow	-	-	-	2	-	-
Harris' Sparrow*	-	-	-	-	-	2
Sparrow, sp.	-	-	-	-	1	1
Dark-eyed Junco, sp.	-	-	-	-	-	-
Slate-colored	-	-	-	-	-	1
White-winged**	-	-	2	-	-	-
Oregon	-	6	-	-	-	1

TABLE IX (CONT.)
JACKSON HOLE, WYOMING
CHRISTMAS BIRD COUNTS 1970 - 1990
Courtesy of the Jackson Hole Bird Club

SPECIES	1970	1974	1978	1982	1986	1990	
Gray-headed Junco**	-	-	-	-	-	-	
Snow Bunting	-	-	-	-	-	3	
Red-winged Blackbird	-	-	-	20	5	1	
Yellow-headed Blackbird*	-	-	-	-	-	-	
Rusty Blackbird**	-	-	-	-	1	-	
Brewer's Blackbird	-	1	14	2	-	-	
Common Grackle*	-	-	-	-	3	-	
Rosy Finch, sp.	-	-	-	-	-	-	
Gray-crowned	-	-	102	150	200	7	
Black	-	-	4	11	CW	CW	
Pine Grosbeak	34	-	4	16	74	30	
Red Crossbill	-	-	-	35^	-	3	
White-winged Crossbill	-	-	-	-	-	-	
Common Redpoll	-	-	3	-	-	-	
Cassin's Finch	-	2	4	3	2	-	-
House Finch*	-	-	-	-	-	1	
Pine Siskin	-	-	11	27	-	1	
American Goldfinch	-	-	-	3	Cw	6	
Evening Grosbeak	-	-	-	1	195	68	
House Sparrow	-	1	129	69	108	34	
Sage Grouse	63	24	15	cw	-	cw	
American Coot	-	-	1	-	-	1	
Killdeer	1	3	2	1	1	1	
Dunlin**	-	-	-	-	-	-	2
Common Snipe	1	9	7	4	3	11	
California Gull*	-	-	-	-	-	-	
Rock Dove	-	-	-	CW	3	CW	
Mourning Dove*	-	-	-	CW^	-	1	
Great Horned Owl	1	-	-	2	1	1	
Snowy Owl*	-	CW	-	-	-	-	
Northern Pygmy-Owl	-	-	-	-	1	-	

SPECIES	1970	1974	1978	1982	1986	1990
Great Gray Owl	-	-	1	-	-	2
Long-eared Owl	-	-	-	-	-	-
Short-eared Owl	-	-	-	-	-	2
Boreal Owl**	-	-	CW	-	-	-
Northern Saw-whet Owl	-	-	CW	CW	-	-
Belted Kingfisher	7	5	10	4	4	12
Yellow-bellied Sapsucker*	-	-	-	-	-	-
Downy Woodpecker	4	10	8	14	12	19
Hairy Woodpecker	12	12	19	13	13	12
Three-toed Woodpecker*	3	-	-	-	-	1
Black-backed Woodpecker*	-	-	-	-	-	-
Northern Flicker	-	-	-	-	-	-
Yellow-shafted*	-	-	-	-	-	-
Red-shafted	-	-	1	1	1	CW
Horned Lark	-	18	175	18	-	2
Gray Jay	9	12	8	10	6	7
Blue Jay	-	-	-	-	-	1
Steller's Jay	3	3	7	18	19	11
Clark's Nutcracker	14	40	23	59	63	54
Black-billed Magpie	89	79	173	97	116	178
American Crow	-	-	3	-	-	-
Common Raven	375	254	339	354	192	289
Black-capped Chickadee	52	150	241^	136	209	197
Mountain Chickadee	41	20	145	108	72	211
Chickadee , sp.	-	-	-	-	-	9
Red-breasted Nuthatch	1	-	2	8	4	2-
White-breasted Nuthatch	5	1	9	14	12	11
Nuthatch, sp.	-	-	-	-	-	3
Brown Creeper	-	1	1	2	6	6

185

TABLE X
RELATIVE ABUNDANCE COUNTS ON THE SNAKE RIVER
MORAN TO WILSON, WYOMING - 40 MILES

BIRD SPECIES	1974 5/4 - 5/5	1979 4/16 - 4/18	1979 5/1 -5/3	1979 5/16 - 5/18
White Pelican	0	0	3	0
Great Blue Heron	18	10	9	21
Trumpeter Swan	0	0	2	0
Canada Goose	140	68	152	108
Green-winged Teal	15	9	9	11
Mallard	134	31	32	21
Gadwall	0	0	0	7
Goldeneye (Common and Barrow's)	20	30	12	2
Common Merganser	126	60	74	36
Osprey	9	4	14	8
Bald Eagle	4	7	7	5
Sharp-shinned Hawk	3	2	0	0
Cooper's Hawk	0	0	1	1
Goshawk	3	0	1	0
Swainson's Hawk	2	0	2	1
Red-tailed Hawk	17	20	13	10
American Kestrel	4	5	11	7
Sandhill Crane	5	14	13	2
Whooping Crane	0	0	0	0
Killdeer	0	3	4	0
Long-billed Curlew	3	0	2	0
California Gull	0	1	0	0
Belted Kingfisher	0	2	5	5
American Crow	0	0	0	?
Common Raven	38	48	40	34

1947 4/24 - 4/26		1979 4/16 - 4/18
862	Duck	130
181	Goose	68
96	White Pelican	0
55	Hawk	27
4	Sandhill Crane	14
0	Trumpeter Swan	0

CHAPTER REFERENCES

INTRODUCTION

Hopkins, Andrew D. 1938. *Bioclimatics, A Science of Life and Climate Relations.* Misc. Publication No. 280, U.S. Dept. of Agriculture, United States Government Printing Office, Washington, D. C.

———. 1920. "Biology—The Bioclimatic Law." *Journal of the Washington Academy of Sciences.* Vol. X. Washington Academy of Science, Washington, D. C.

Chapman, Royal N. 1931. *Animal Ecology.* McGraw-Hill Book Co. Inc., New York and London.

Weaver, John E., and Frederick E. Clements. 1938. *Plant Ecology.* McGraw Hill Book Co., New York and London.

FEBRUARY 27—MARCH 5

Bent, Arthur Cleveland, 1946. *Life Histories of North American Jays, Crows and Titmice.* United States National Museum Bulletin 191, Order Passeriformes, Smithsonian Institution, Washington D.C.

Heinrich, Bernd. 1989. *Ravens In Winter.* Simon and Schuster, New York.

Peterson, R.T. 1961. *A Field Guide to Western Birds.* Houghton Mifflin Co., Boston.

National Geographic Society, 1983. *Field Guide to the Birds of North America.* Washington, D.C.

Turner, John. 1971. *The Magnificent Bald Eagle.* Random House, New York.

———. Sept. 1991. "Eagles Over Wyoming." *Wyoming Wildlife.*

MARCH 6—12

Craighead, John J., Frank C. Craighead, Jr. and Ray J. Davis. 1963. *A Field Guide to Rocky Mountain Wild Flowers.* Houghton Mifflin Co., Boston.

Dorn, Robert D. 1988. *Vascular Plants of Wyoming.* Mountain West Publishing, Cheyenne, Wyoming.

Petrides, G.A. 1958. *A Field Guide to Trees and Shrubs.* Houghton Mifflin Co., Boston.

Sargent, Charles Sprague. 1965. *Manual of the Trees of North America.* Dover Publications, Inc., New York.

Warren, E.T.M. 1988. *Creating A Butterfly Garden.* Henry Holt and Company, Inc., New York.

MARCH 13—19

Craighead, F.C. Jr., John J. Craighead, Charles E. Cote, Helmut K. Buechner. 1972. *Satellite and Ground Radiotracking of Elk. Animal Orientation and Navigation.* NASA Scientific and Technical Information Office, Washington, D.C.

Bent, Arthur Cleveland. 1937. *Life Histories of North American Birds of Prey.* United States National Museum Bulletin 167, Order Falconiformes (Part I), Smithsonian Institution, Washington, D.C.

———. 1937. *Life Histories of North American Birds of Prey.* United States National Museum Bulletin 170, Order Falconiformes and Strigiformes (Part II), Smithsonian Institution, Washington, D.C.

MARCH 20—26

Borror, Donald J., and Richard E. White. 1970. *A Field Guide to Insects.* Houghton Mifflin Co., Boston.

Van Vleck, Sarita. 1977. *Growing Wings.* William L. Banhan Publisher, Dublin, New Hampshire.

MARCH 27—APRIL 2

Craighead, Frank C., and David Mindell. 1981. *Nesting Raptors in Western Wyoming 1947 and 1975.* The Journal of Wildlife Management, Vol. 45, No. 4. The Wildlife Society, Inc., Washington, D.C.

Craighead, Frank C., and John J. Craighead. 1950. *The Ecology of Raptor Predation.* Transactions of the Fifteenth North American Wildlife Conference, Wildlife Management Institute, Washington, D.C.

———. Craighead. 1956. *Hawks, Owls and Wildlife.* The Stackpole Company, Harrisburg, Pennsylvania and Wildlife Management Institute, Washington, D.C.

Daubenmire, R.F. 1947. *Plants and Environment.* John Wiley and Sons, Inc., New York.

Hopkins, Andrew D. 1919. *The Bioclimatic Law as Applied to Entomological and Farm Practice.* The Scientific Monthly, Vol. VIII. 1919, Science Press, New York.

APRIL 3—9

Craighead, Frank C. Jr., and John J. Craighead. 1949. "Nesting Canada Geese on the Upper Snake River." *The Journal of Wildlife Management,* Vol. 13, No.1.

Craighead, John J. 1950. *A Biological and Economic Appraisal of the Jackson Hole Elk Herd.* New York Zoological Society, New York.

Harrison, H. Hal. 1975. *A Field Guide to Bird's Nests.* Houghton Mifflin Co., Boston.

Murie, Olaus J. 1951. *The Elk of North America.* Stackpole Co. and Wildlife Management Institute, Washington, D.C.

———. 1979. *Nature Guide to Jackson Hole.* Teton Bookshop, Jackson, Wyoming.

APRIL 10—16

Craighead, Frank C. Jr., and John J. Craighead. "Grizzly Bear Prehibernation and Denning Activities as Determined by Radio-tracking," *Wildlife Monographs* 32. The Wildlife Society. 1972. Washington, D.C.

Craighead, Frank C. Jr. 1979. *Track of the Grizzly.* Sierra Club Press, San Francisco.

————. 1974. "Grizzly Bear Ranges and Movement as Determined by Radiotracking." *Bears—Their Biology and Management.* IUCN, Morges, Switzerland.

Craighead, John J., and Frank C. Craighead. 1970. "Grizzly Bear-Man Relationships in Yellowstone National Park." *Bears—Their Biology and Management.* IUCN, Morges, Switzerland.

Craighead, John J., and Joel R. Varney and Frank C. Craighead, Jr. 1974. "A Population Analysis of the Yellowstone Grizzly Bears." Bulletin 40. Montana Forest and Conservation Station, School of Forestry, University of Montana, Missoula, Montana.

APRIL 17—23

Craighead, John J., Frank C. Craighead and Ray J. Davis. 1963. *A Field Guide to Rocky Mountain Wild Flowers.* Houghton Mifflin Co., Boston.

McEneaney, Terry. 1988. *Birds of Yellowstone.* Roberts Rinehart, Inc., Boulder, Colorado.

Raynes, Bert. 1984. *Birds of Grand Teton National Park and the Surrounding Area.* Grand Teton Natural History Association, Moose, Wyoming.

Stokes, Donald W., and Lillian Q. Stokes. 1983. *A Guide to Bird Behavior.* Stokes Nature Guides, Vol. 2. Little Brown and Co., Boston.

————. 1989. *A Guide to Bird Behavior.* Stokes Nature Guides, Vol. 3. Little Brown and Co., Boston.

APRIL 24—30

Angier, Bradford. 1969. *Feasting Free on Wild Edibles.* Stackpole Books, Harrisburg, Pennsylvania.

————. 1974. *Field Guide to Edible Wild Plants.* Stackpole Books, Harrisburg, Pennsylvania.

Ericksen-Brown, Charlotte. 1979. *Use of Plants for the Past 500 Years.* Hunter Rose Co. Ltd., Toronto, Canada.

Patterson, Robert L. 1952. *The Sage Grouse in Wyoming.* Wyoming Game and Fish Commission. Sage Books, Inc., Denver.

Sturtevant, Edward Lewis. 1919. *Sturtevant's Notes on Edible Plants.* Edited by V.P. Hedrick. J.B. Lyon Company, Albany, New York.

MAY 1—7

Autenrieth, Robert E., and Edson Fichter. 1975. "On the Behavior and Socialization of Pronghorn Fawns." *Wildlife Monographs.* No. 42. The Wildlife Society, Wash. D.C.

Miller, Erston V. 1953. *Within the Living Plant.* The Blakiston Company Inc., New York.

Robbins, S. Chandler, Bertel Bruun and Herbert S. Zim. 1966. *Birds of North America.* Golden Press, New York.

MAY 8—14

Bent, Arthur Cleveland. 1939. *Life Histories of North American Wild Fowl.* Vol. II. Dover Publications, Inc., New York.

Stefferud, Alfred, and Arnold Nelson. 1966. *Birds In Our Lives.* United States Government Printing Office, Washington, D.C. (J. & F. Craighead, Raptors, pp.200-217.)

Terres, K. John. 1987. *The Audubon Society Encyclopedia of North American Birds.* Alfred A. Knopf, New York.

MAY 15—21

McKenny, Margaret, and Daniel E. Stuntz. 1971. *The Savory Wild Mushroom.* The University of Washington Press, Seattle and London.

Smith, Alexander H. 1971. *The Mushroom Hunter's Field Guide.* The University of Michigan Press, Ann Arbor, Michigan.

MAY 22—28

Porsild, A. E. l974. *Rocky Mountain Wild Flowers.* National Museums of Natural Sciences, National Museums of Canada, Ottawa, Canada.

Range Plant Handbook. 1937. U.S. Forest Service, U.S. Government Printing Office, Washington, D.C.

Tilden, J.W., and Arthur C. Smith. 1986. *A Field Guide to Western Butterflies.* Houghton Mifflin Co., Boston.

Whitson, Tom D. (editor). 1987. *Weeds and Poisonous Plants of Wyoming and Utah.* Cooperative Extension Service, College of Agriculture, University of Wyoming, Laramie.

JUNE 5 -11

Hines, Bob. 1978. *Ducks at a Distance.* Dept. of the Interior, U.S. Fish & Wildlife Service, Washington, D.C.

Kluck, Tom, Howard Funk and Charles Stulzenbaker. 1974. *Waterfowl Identification in the Central Flyway.* Wyoming Game and Fish Dept., Cheyenne, Wyoming.

Varley, John D., and Paul Schullery. l983. *Freshwater Wilderness.* The Yellowstone Library and Museum Association, Yellowstone National Park.

JUNE 12—18

Bryan, Harry, and Willard E. Dilley. 1972. *Wildlife of Yellowstone and Grand Teton National Parks.* Wheelwright Lithographing Co., Salt Lake City, Utah.

Craighead, Karen. *Large Mammals of Yellowstone and Teton National Parks.* Walker Press, Paris, Canada.

JUNE 19—25

Burt, William Henry, and Richard Philip Grossenheider. 1976. *A Field Guide to the Mammals, North America North of Mexico.* Houghton Mifflin Co., Boston.

James, Wilma Roberts. 1973. *Know Your Poisonous Plants*. Naturegraph Publishers Inc., Happy Camp, California.

JUNE 26—JULY 2

Craighead, Frank C. 1951. *A Biological and Economic Evaluation of Coyote Predation*. New York Zoological Society and the Conservation Foundation, New York.

Fitch, H.S., and J. R. Bentley. 1949. *Use of California Annual-plant Forage by Range Rodents*. *Ecology*. Vol. 30, No.3.

Hafele, Rick, and Dave Hughes. 1981. *The Complete Book of Western Hatches*. Frank Amato Publications, Portland, Oregon.

O'Toole, Christopher (Editor). 1986. *The Encyclopedia of Insects*. Equinox (Oxford), Ltd. Facts on File Inc., New York.

Schwiebert, G. Ernest, Jr. 1955. *Matching the Hatch*. Stoeger Publishing Company, South Hackensack, New Jersey.

Tilden, J.W., and Arthur C. Smith. 1986. *A Field Guide to Western Butterflies*. Houghton Mifflin Co. Boston.

JULY 3—9

Jelks, Mary. *Allergy Plants*. World-Wide Publications, Tampa, Florida.

Scott, Oliver K. 1991. *Check List—Birds of Wyoming*. 5120 Alcova Rt., Box 16, Casper, Wyoming.

Paige, Ken N. "The Wiliest Wildflower in the West," *Natural History*. June 88.

JULY 10—16

Spackman, Everett W., and Fred A. Lawson. *Insects and Related Pests of Trees, Shrubs and Lawns*. College of Agriculture Cooperative Extension Service, University of Wyoming, Laramie.

JULY 17-23

Angier, Bradford. *Field Guide to Edible Wild Plants*. 1974. Stackpole Books, Harrisburg, Pennsylvania.

Stokes, Donald and Lillian. *A Guide to Bird Behavior*. 1989. Little, Brown and Company, Boston.

Turner, Nancy J. *Food Plants of British Columbian Indians*. 1975. British Columbia Provincial Museum, Victoria, Canada.

JULY 24—30

Craighead, Frank C., Jr., and John J. Craighead. Revised by Ray E. Smith and D. Shiras Jarvis. *How to Survive on Land and Sea*. 1984. Naval Institute Press, Annapolis, Maryland.

VanVleck, Sarita. 1977. *Growing Wings, the Perennial Cycle of Bird Life*. William L. Bauhan, Publisher, Dublin, New Hampshire.

JULY 31—AUGUST 6
Scotter, George W., and Halle Flygare. 1986. *Wildflowers of the Canadian Rockies.* Hurtig Publishers, Edmonton, Canada.

AUGUST 7—13
Petersen, Lee. 1978. *A Field Guide to Edible Wild Plants.* Houghton Mifflin Co., Boston.

AUGUST 14—20
Heller, Christine A. 1973. *Wild Edible and Poisonous Plants of Alaska.* Publication #40. Cooperative Extension Service, University of Alaska.

AUGUST 21—27
Brooks, C.E.P. *Climate Through the Ages.* Dover Publications, Inc., New York.

Clark, Tim W., and Mark R. Stromberg. 1987. *Mammals in Wyoming.* Museum of Natural History, Lawrence, Kansas.

Hopkins, Andrew D. 1921. *Bioclimatics. Journal of the Washington Academy of Sciences,* Vol. II. Washington Academy of the Sciences, Washington, D.C.

SEPTEMBER 4—10
Craighead, Frank C. 1951. *A Biological and Economic Evaluation of Coyote Predation.* The New York Zoological Society. The Conservation Foundation, New York.

Houston, Douglas B. 1968. *The Shiras Moose in Jackson Hole, Wyoming.* Natural History Society of Grand Teton National Park, Moose, Wyoming.

SEPTEMBER 18—24
Clark, William S., and Brian Wheeler. 1987. *A Field Guide to Hawks.* The Peterson Field Guide Series. Houghton Mifflin, Co., Boston.

NOVEMBER 6—12
Lyman, Charles P., and Albert R. Dawe. 1960. "Mammalian Hibernation," *Bulletin of the Museum of Comparative Zoology.* Harvard College, Vol. 124, Cambridge, Massachusetts.

NOVEMBER 20—26
Christmas Bird Counts. 1970-1990. Jackson Hole, Wyoming.

Jackson Hole Bird Club. 1990. *Jackson Hole Bird Club Christmas Bird Count.* December 15, 1990. Jackson Hole, Wyoming.

DECEMBER 4—31
Murie, Olaus J. 1954. *A Field Guide to Animal Tracks.* Houghton Mifflin Co., Boston.

ADDITIONAL REFERENCES
(GENERAL TO BOOK)

Bauer, Erwin A. 1983. *Deer in Their World*. Stackpole Books, Harrisburg, Pennsylvania.

Billings, W.D. 1964. *Plants and the Ecosystem*. Wadsworth Publishing Company, Inc., Belmont, California.

Bird, David M. 1983. *Biology and Management of Bald Eagles and Ospreys*. Harpell Press, Quebec, Canada.

Birds of Gray's Lake National Wildlife Refuge. 1988. U.S. Fish and Wildlife Service, Wyan, Idaho.

Borger, Gary A. 1944. *Naturals, A Guide to Food Organisms of the Trout*. Stackpole Books, Harrisburg, Pennsylvania.

Brown, Charles R., and Mary B. Brown. 1990. "The Great Egg Scramble," *Natural History*. February 1990.

Call, Mayo W. 1978. *Nesting Habitats and Surveying Techniques for Common Western Raptors*. Bureau of Land Management, Denver Service Center, Denver, Colorado.

Clark, Tim W. 1981. *Ecology of Jackson Hole, Wyoming, A Primer*. T. W. Clark, Box 2705, Jackson, Wyoming.

Clark, William S., and Brian K. Wheeler. 1987. *A Field Guide to Hawks*. Houghton Mifflin Co., Boston.

Dannen, Kent, and Donna Dannen. 1981. *Rocky Mountain Wildflowers*. Tundra Publications, Estes Park, Colorado.

Davis, Ray J. 1952. *Flora of Idaho*. William C. Brown Company, Dubuque, Iowa.

Dobie, Frank J. 1947. *The Voice of the Coyote*. University of Nebraska Press, Lincoln, Nebraska, and London.

Dorn, Jane L., and Robert D. Dorn. "Wyoming Birds." Mountain West Publishing, Cheyenne, Wyoming.

Farrand, John Jr. 1991. *Familiar Insects and Spiders, North America*. The Audubon Society Pocket Guides, Alfred A Knopf, Inc., New York.

Harmata, Al, and Bob Oakleaf. 1992. *Bald Eagles in the Greater Yellowstone Ecosystem: An Ecological Study with Emphasis on the Snake River, Wyoming*. Montana State University, Bozeman, Montana, and Wyoming Game and Fish Department, Lander, Wyoming.

Harris, Peter, and L.T. Kok. 1986. "Biological Control of Carduus Thistles with Trichosirocalus Horridus." Research Station, Agriculture Canada, Communications Branch, Ottawa.

Johnsguard, Paul A. 1982. *Teton Wildlife*. Colorado Associated University Press, Boulder, Colorado.

Juracek, John, and Craig Mathews. 1992. *Fishing Yellowstone Hatched*. Blue Ribbon Flies, West Yellowstone, Montana.

Kormandy, Edward J. 1969. *Concepts of Ecology*. Prentice-Hall, Inc., Englewood Cliffs, New Jersey.

Leydet, Francois. 1988. *The Coyote*. University of Oklahoma Press, Norman, Oklahoma, and London.

Lindley, John, and Thomas Moore, editors. 1876. *The Treasury of Botany*, Vol. II. Longmans, Green and Co., London.

Lyman, Charles P., and Albert R. Dawe. 1960. "Mammalian Hibernation," *Bulletin of the Museum of Comparative Zoology*. Harvard College, Vol. 124. Cambridge, Massachusetts.

Martin, Alexander, Zim and Nelson. 1951. *American Wildlife and Plants*. McGraw-Hill Book Co. Inc., New York.

McDougall, W.B., and Herma A. Baggley. 1956. *Plants of Yellowstone National Park*. Yellowstone Library and Museum Association, Yellowstone Park, Wyoming.

Murie, Adolf. 1940. "Ecology of the Coyote in the Yellowstone," *Conservation Bulletin*. No. 4. U.S. Printing Office.

Murie, O. J. 1935. "Food Habits of the Coyote in Jackson Hole, Wyoming," *U.S. Dept. of Agriculture Circular*. No. 362.

Murie, Olaus J. 1954. *A Field Guide to Animal Tracks*. Houghton Mifflin Co., Boston.

Peterson, Roger T. 1961. *A Field Guide to Western Birds*. Houghton Mifflin Co., Boston.

Podolsky, Alexander S. 1984. *New Phenology*. John Wiley and Sons.

Poritz, Noah and Leona. 1992. *Biological Control of Weeds*. 1140 Cherry Drive, Bozeman, Montana 59715.

Raynes, Bert and Meg. 1984. *Checklist, Birds in Jackson Hole*. Grand Teton Natural History Association.

Rickett, Harold William. 1973. *Wildflowers of the United States, the Central Mountains and Plains*. Vol.VI, Parts 1, 2, and 3. New York Botanical Gardens, McGraw-Hill Book Co., New York.

Scott, Oliver K. 1993. *A Birder's Guide to Wyoming*. American Birding Association Sales. Colorado Springs, Colorado.

Shaw, Richard J. 1976. *Field Guide to the Vascular Plants of Grand Teton National Park and Teton County, Wyoming*. Utah State University Press, Logan, Utah.

194

————. 1964. *Trees and Flowering Shrubs of Yellowstone and Grand Teton National Parks.* The Wheelwright Press, Salt Lake City, Utah.

————. 1992. *Vascular Plants of Grand Teton National Park and Teton County. An Annotated Checklist.* Grand Teton Natural History Association, Grand Teton National Park, Moose, Wyoming.

Smith, Robert H. 1984. *Native Trout of North America.* Frank Amato Publications, Portland, Oregon.

Stokes, Donald W. 1979, 1983, 1989. *A Guide to the Behavior of Common Birds.* Volumes I, II, and III. Little, Brown and Company, Boston and Toronto.

Temple, Stanley A. 1977. *Endangered Birds, Management Techniques for Preserving Threatened Species.* The University of Wisconsin Press, Madison, Wisconsin.

Terres, John. 1987. *The Audubon Society Encyclopedia of North American Birds.* Alfred A. Knopf, New York.

Wallen, R.L. 1991. "Annual Variation in Harlequin Duck Population Size, Productivity and Fidelity to Grand Teton National Park." Office of Science and Resource Management, Grand Teton National Park, Moose, Wyoming.

Walton, Richard K., and Paul A. Opler. 1990. *Familiar Butterflies, North America.* The Audubon Society Pocket Guides, Alfred A. Knopf, Inc., New York.

Whitney, Stephen. 1992. *Western Forests.* The Audubon Society Nature Guides, Alfred A. Knopf, Inc., New York.

Wyoming Bird Checklist, Wyoming Game and Fish Dept., Lander, Wyoming.

INDEX

198

ABOUT THE AUTHOR

Dr. Frank C. Craighead Jr., a Wyoming resident from 1947 until his death in 2001, was one of America's most distinguished field biologists. He wrote or co-authored more than seventy-five technical and popular articles, many of which appeared in *National Geographic.* His books include *Hawks Owls and Wildlife,* and the *Peterson Field Guide to Rocky Mountain Wildflowers.* Dr. Craighead's *Track of the Grizzly* created public awareness over the plight of the grizzly in the Yellowstone ecosystem and made Dr. Craighead's name synonymous with grizzly bears.

Dr. Craighead received many honors and awards in more than fifty years of wildlife research and conservation. In 1988 he was one of fifteen people throughout the world honored with the National Geographic Centennial Award. In a pioneering conservation effort, Frank and his twin brother, John, were instrumental in developing the Wild and Scenic Rivers concept. They also pioneered the development and use of radio telemetry for tracking and studying large mammals, including grizzly, black bear, and elk, in the Yellowstone ecosystem.

Dr. Craighead continued to study the natural world and to speak out for the conservation of wilderness throughout his life. His wife, Shirley, still lives in Moose, Wyoming, where the two spent so many years discovering the beauty of Grand Teton National Park.